THE TIMES

Famous Passages from
Spiritual Writings

THE TIMES

Famous Passages from Spiritual Writings

COMPILED BY OWEN COLLINS

Fount
An Imprint of HarperCollins*Publishers*

Fount is an Imprint of
HarperCollins*Religious*
part of HarperCollins*Publishers*
77–85 Fulham Palace Road, London W6 8JB
www.**fire**and**water**.com

First published in Great Britain in 2000 by Fount

1 3 5 7 9 10 8 6 4 2

Compilation Copyright © 2000 Owen Collins

Owen Collins asserts the moral right to be identified
as the compiler of this work.

A catalogue record for this book is available
from the British Library.

ISBN 0 00 710226 7

Printed and bound in Great Britain by
Omnia Books Limited, Glasgow

CONTENTS

✿ Dreams and Visions 59

INTRODUCTION

꩜

This book has been divided into twelve sections that reflect the rich variety in both content and style displayed in the works of Christian spiritual writers: spiritual instruction; visions and dreams; sermons and lectures; martyrs and martyrdoms; rules and catechisms; commentaries; letters; conversion stories; journals, diaries, biographies and autobiographies; allegories and stories; poetry; and hymns. In each section the material is arranged chronologically, according to the death date of the author.

There are extracts from the works of over sixty writers in this collection. Many of the more well-known, such as Aquinas, Augustine, Baxter, Bernard of Clairvaux, Bunyan, Calvin, Cowper, the author of *The Cloud of Unknowing*, Donne, Jonathan Edwards, George Fox, John Foxe, Francis of Sales, Matthew Henry, George Herbert, Hilton, Ignatius of Loyola, John of the Cross, Julian of Norwich, Thomas à Kempis, Brother Lawrence, Luther, Newman, Pascal, Rolle, Ryle, Spurgeon, and John and Charles Wesley are represented. There are also a number of less well-known, even half-forgotten, spiritual writers here: Brainerd, Catherine of Siena, Chrysostom, John Colet, Ephraem the Syrian, Fénelon, August Hermann Franke, Madame Guyon,

Ignatius of Antioch, Margery Kempe, Charles Kingsley, Leo I, Teresa of Avila and the author of *Theologia Germanica*.

A number of the extracts have been chosen because they were the favourite of some influential Christian. One example of this is *Theologia Germanica*, an almost forgotten book until it was redis-covered and published in 1516 by Martin Luther. Luther kept it by his bedside, and said of it, 'Next to the Bible and St Augustine, no book has ever come into my hands from which I have learnt more of God and Christ, and man and all things that are.'

One of the longest extracts in this collection is from Luther's *Preface to the Epistle to the Romans*, which originated as Luther's lecture notes to his theological students at Wittenberg. He deliv-ered these lectures in 1515 when he was on fire with his person-al discovery of what 'the just shall live by faith' (Romans 1:17) meant. This example from Luther's voluminous writings may be remembered by anyone who recalls the details of John Wesley's conversion. A brief account of the moment when Wesley found that his heart 'was strangely warmed' after hearing Luther's *Preface to the Epistle to the Romans* being read is included in this collec-tion, taken from the entry in Wesley's *Journal* for 24 May 1738.

The two extracts from *The Cloud of Unknowing* (pp. 10–11) and the two extracts from Augustine (pp. 142, 149) reflect the dif-ferent renderings of these writers which exist today. In both cases there is one example of a more traditional translation and one example of a more contemporary translation.

One extract from Bernard, Abbot of Clairvaux, is included in the collection. It is taken from *The Song of Songs*, a lengthy col-lection of eighty-six sermons all related to the spiritual life of men and women, and among the most beautiful examples of medieval scriptural exegesis. Bernard, author of several mystical works and a monastic Rule, sought, above all and in all, to be with God and to bring all people to experience God. In their own different ways all the other contributors in this collection, which ranges over the first two millennia, have attempted to do the same. They have left in their labours a rich heritage of Christian writing from which we may all benefit.

OWEN COLLINS

SPIRITUAL INSTRUCTION

~∞~

The Sermon on the Mount

MATTHEW 5:1–48 AV

∞And seeing the multitudes, he went up into a mountain: and when he was set, his disciples came unto him:

And he opened his mouth, and taught them, saying,

Blessed are the poor in spirit: for theirs is the kingdom of heaven.

Blessed are they that mourn: for they shall be comforted.

Blessed are the meek: for they shall inherit the earth.

Blessed are they which do hunger and thirst after righteousness: for they shall be filled.

Blessed are the merciful: for they shall obtain mercy.

Blessed are the pure in heart: for they shall see God.

Blessed are the peacemakers: for they shall be called the children of God.

Blessed are they which are persecuted for righteousness' sake: for theirs is the kingdom of heaven.

Blessed are ye, when men shall revile you, and persecute you, and shall say all manner of evil against you falsely, for my sake.

Rejoice, and be exceeding glad: for great is your reward in heaven: for so persecuted they the prophets which were before you.

Ye are the salt of the earth: but if the salt have lost his savour, wherewith shall it be salted? it is thenceforth good for nothing, but to be cast out, and to be trodden under foot of men. Ye are the light of the world. A city that is set on an hill cannot be hid. Neither do men light a candle, and put it under a bushel, but on a candlestick; and it giveth light unto all that are in the house. Let your light so shine before men, that they may see your good works, and glorify your Father which is in heaven. Think not that I am come to destroy the law, or the prophets: I am not come to destroy, but to fulfil. For verily I say unto you, Till heaven and earth pass, one jot or one tittle shall in no wise pass from the law, till all be fulfilled.

Whosoever therefore shall break one of these least commandments, and shall teach men so, he shall be called the least in the kingdom of heaven: but whosoever shall do and teach them, the same shall be called great in the kingdom of heaven.

For I say unto you, That except your righteousness shall exceed the righteousness of the scribes and Pharisees, ye shall in no case enter into the kingdom of heaven.

Ye have heard that it was said of them of old time, Thou shalt not kill; and whosoever shall kill shall be in danger of the judgment: But I say unto you, That whosoever is angry with his brother without a cause shall be in danger of the judgment: and whosoever shall say to his brother, Raca, shall be in danger of the council: but whosoever shall say, Thou fool, shall be in danger of hell fire.

Therefore if thou bring thy gift to the altar, and there rememberest that thy brother hath ought against thee; Leave there thy gift before the altar, and go thy way; first be reconciled to thy brother, and then come and offer thy gift. Agree with thine adversary quickly, whiles thou art in the way with him; lest at any time the adversary deliver thee to the judge, and the judge deliver thee to the officer, and thou be cast into prison. Verily I say unto thee, Thou shalt by no means come out thence, till thou hast paid the uttermost farthing.

Ye have heard that it was said by them of old time, Thou shalt not commit adultery: But I say unto you, That whosoever looketh on a woman to lust after her hath committed adultery with her already in his heart. And if thy right eye offend thee, pluck it out, and cast it from thee: for it is profitable for thee that one of thy members should perish, and not that thy whole body should be cast into hell. And if thy right hand offend thee, cut it off, and cast it from thee: for it is profitable for thee that one of thy members should perish, and not that thy whole body should be cast into hell. It hath been said, Whosoever shall put away his wife, let him give her a writing of divorcement: But I say unto you, That whosoever shall put away his wife, saving for the cause of fornication, causeth her to commit adultery: and whosoever shall marry her that is divorced committeth adultery.

Again, ye have heard that it hath been said by them of old time, Thou shalt not forswear thyself, but shalt perform unto the Lord thine oaths: But I say unto you, Swear not at all; neither by heaven; for it is God's throne: Nor by the earth; for it is his footstool: neither by Jerusalem; for it is the city of the great King. Neither shalt thou swear by thy head, because thou canst not make one hair white or black. But let your communication be, Yea, yea; Nay, nay: for whatsoever is more than these cometh of evil.

Ye have heard that it hath been said, An eye for an eye, and a tooth for a tooth: But I say unto you, That ye resist not evil: but whosoever shall smite thee on thy right cheek, turn to him the other also. And if any man will sue thee at the law, and take away thy coat, let him have thy cloak also. And whosoever shall compel thee to go a mile, go with him twain. Give to him that asketh thee, and from him that would borrow of thee turn not thou away. Ye have heard that it hath been said, Thou shalt love thy neighbour, and hate thine enemy. But I say unto you, Love your enemies, bless them that curse you, do good to them that hate you, and pray for them which despitefully use you, and persecute you; That ye may be the children of your Father which is in heaven: for he maketh his sun to rise on the evil and on the good, and sendeth rain on the just and on the unjust. For if ye love them which love you, what reward have ye? do not even the publicans the same? And if ye salute your brethren only, what do ye more than others? do not even the publicans so? Be ye therefore perfect, even as your Father which is in heaven is perfect.

The greatest of these is charity

I CORINTHIANS 13:1–13 AV

◁ Though I speak with the tongues of men and of angels, and have not charity, I am become as sounding brass, or a tinkling cymbal. And though I have the gift of prophecy, and understand all mysteries, and all knowledge; and though I have all faith, so that I could remove mountains, and have not charity, I am nothing. And though I bestow all my goods to feed the poor, and though I give my body to be burned, and have not charity, it profiteth me nothing. Charity suffereth long, and is kind; charity envieth not; charity vaunteth not itself, is not puffed up, Doth not behave itself unseemly, seeketh not her own, is not easily provoked, thinketh no evil; Rejoiceth not in iniquity, but rejoiceth in the truth; Beareth all things, believeth all things, hopeth all things, endureth all things. Charity never faileth: but whether there be prophecies, they shall fail; whether there be tongues, they shall cease; whether there be knowledge, it shall vanish away. For we know in part, and we prophesy in part. But when that which is perfect is come, then that which is in part shall be done away. When I was a child, I spake as a child, I understood as a child, I thought as a child: but when I became a man, I put away childish things. For now we see through a glass, darkly; but then face to face: now I know in part; but then shall I know even as also I am known. And now abideth faith, hope, charity, these three; but the greatest of these is charity.

Is joy a virtue?

THOMAS AQUINAS, *SUMMA THEOLOGIAE*

∽ *Objection 1*: It would seem that joy is a virtue. For vice is contrary to virtue. Now sorrow is set down as a vice, as in the case of sloth and envy. Therefore joy also should be accounted a virtue.

∽ *Objection 2*: Further, as love and hope are passions, the object of which is 'good', so also is joy. Now love and hope are reckoned to be virtues. Therefore joy also should be reckoned a virtue.

∽ *Objection 3*: Further, the precepts of the Law are about acts of virtue. But we are commanded to rejoice in the Lord, according to Philippians 4:4: 'Rejoice in the Lord always.' Therefore joy is a virtue.

∽ *On the contrary*, It is not numbered among the theological virtues, nor among the moral, nor among the intellectual virtues.

∽ *I answer that*, Virtue is an operative habit, wherefore by its very nature it has an inclination to a certain act. Now it may happen that from the same habit there proceed several ordinate and homogeneous acts, each of which follows from another. And since the subsequent acts do not proceed from the virtuous habit except through the preceding act, hence it is that the virtue is defined and named in reference to that preceding act, although those other acts also proceed from the virtue. Love is the first affection of the appetitive power, and that desire and joy follow from it. Hence the same virtuous habit inclines us to love and desire the beloved good, and to rejoice in it. But in as much as love is the first of these acts, that virtue takes its name, not from joy, nor from desire, but from love, and is called charity. Hence joy is not a virtue distinct from charity, but an act, or effect, of charity: for which reason it is numbered among the Fruits (Galatians 5:22).

∽*Reply to Objection 1*: The sorrow which is a vice is caused by inordinate self-love, and this is not a special vice, but a general source of the vices, so that it was necessary to account certain particular sorrows as special vices, because they do not arise from a special, but from a general vice. On the other hand love of God is accounted a special virtue, namely charity, to which joy must be referred, as its proper act.

∽*Reply to Objection 2*: Hope proceeds from love even as joy does, but hope adds, on the part of the object, a special character, viz. 'difficult', and 'possible to obtain'; for which reason it is accounted a special virtue. On the other hand joy does not add to love any special aspect, that might cause a special virtue.

∽*Reply to Objection 3*: The Law prescribes joy, as being an act of charity, albeit not its first act.

Prayer and meditation

RICHARD ROLLE, *THE FIRE OF LOVE*
∽God knows all things. He knows what we wish even before we ask for it. Yet we must pray, for many reasons. But first

because Christ set us an example: he went up into the mountains alone at night to pray. And also because the apostles tell us to pray: 'Pray continually' (1 Thessalonians 5:17), and men ought always to pray and not give up (see Luke 18:1). But we ought to pray to acquire grace for this life and glory in the next. So we are told, 'For everyone who asks receives; he who seeks finds; and to him who knocks, the door will be opened' (Luke 11:10). Again, we pray because angels offer our prayers to God to help their fulfilment.

Thoughts and desires are indeed naked and open to God alone. Yet angels know when saints think worthy and holy things. They know when they are inflamed by the love of eternal life; God reveals it to them, and our outward acts display who serves God alone. That is why the angel said to Daniel, 'You are a man of strong desires' (Daniel 9:23 Vulgate). We should also pray because in constant prayer the soul is ignited with the fire of divine love. Our Lord speaks truly through the prophet, 'Is not my word like fire ... and like a hammer that breaks a rock in pieces?' (Jeremiah 23:29). And the psalmist says, 'Your speech is a burning fire' (Psalm 119:140 Vulgate).

Closeness to God

RICHARD ROLLE, *THE FIRE OF LOVE*

৩The closer and more present God is to a soul, the purer is his love. This is how one rejoices more purely in God. He feels more strongly God's goodness and loving-kindness which is bound to be poured out in those who love him. With incomparable joy it fills to overflowing the hearts of the just.

With great purity the spirit is totally established in a single desire for eternity, and looks up continually, with freedom, towards heavenly things. It is so caught up that it is ravished from every other thing to which it does not turn and cannot love.

But this ravishing, however, is clearly to be understood in two ways. In one way, he is so ravished out of bodily feeling that at the time of rapture he cannot feel whatever is done in or from the flesh. He is not, however, dead, but alive, because the soul yet quickens the body. In this way the saints and the elect are sometimes enraptured for the benefit and instruction of others, as Paul was ravished in the third heaven. In this way too sinners are sometimes ravished so that they may see the joy of the blessed or the punishments of the damned, in order that they themselves or others may be corrected. And we read of many such examples.

In the other way, it is called the rapture of the raising of the mind to God by contemplation. This is found in all the perfect lovers of God, and in no one unless they love God. It is correctly called rapture or ravishing, like the other, because it does a certain violence, as it were, against nature. Moreover, it is truly supernatural, since it may change a man from a vile sinner to a son of God, who is carried up into God, full of spiritual joy.

The means which the soul takes to arrive at pure and generous love

CATHERINE OF SIENA, *TREATISE ON DIVINE PROVIDENCE*

✧When the soul has passed through the doctrine of Christ crucified, with true love of virtue and hatred of vice, and has arrived at the house of self-knowledge and entered therein, she remains, with her door barred, in watching and constant prayer, separated entirely from the consolations of the world. Why does she thus shut herself in? She does so from fear, knowing her own imperfections, and also from the desire, which she has, of arriving at pure and generous love. And because she sees and knows well that in no other way can she arrive thereat, she waits, with a lively faith for My arrival, through increase of grace in her. How is a lively faith to be recognized? By perseverance in virtue, and by the fact that the soul never turns back for anything, whatever it be, nor rises from holy prayer, for any reason except (note well) for obedience or charity's sake. For no other reason ought she to leave off prayer, for, during the time ordained for prayer, the Devil is wont to arrive in the soul, causing much more conflict and trouble than when the soul is not occupied in prayer. This he does in order that holy prayer may become tedious to the soul, tempting her often with these words: *This prayer avails you nothing, for you need attend to nothing except your vocal prayers*. He acts thus in order that, becoming wearied and confused in mind, she may abandon the exercise of prayer, which is a weapon with which the soul can defend herself from every adversary, if grasped with the hand of love, by the arm of free choice in the light of the Holy Faith.

The song of angels

WALTER HILTON, *THE SCALE OF PERFECTION*
Then the devil left him [Jesus], and angels came and attended him (Matthew 4:11)

᳇ When a soul is purified by the love of God, illumined by wisdom, stabled by the might of God, then is the eye of the soul opened to view spiritual things, such as angels and heavenly beings. Then the purified soul is able to feel the touch and hear the voice of good angels. This feeling and hearing is not bodily but spiritual. For when the soul is lifted up and ravished out of sensuality, and away from all earthly things, then in great fervour and light (if our Lord wills) the soul may hear and feel heavenly sound, made by the presence of angels as they love God. This is the song of the angels.

For the sovereign and essential joy is in the love of God by himself and for himself. Following this, and secondly, comes the communing and viewing angels and heavenly beings. So whoever wishes to hear the angel's song must take care not to delude himself, to give himself over to his own imagination or to be deceived by the devil. It is necessary for him to have perfect love. This occurs when all vain love, fear, joy and sorrow is thrown out of the heart, so that it only loves God, only fears God, and only derives joy and sorrow from God.

This work of contemplation

THE CLOUD OF UNKNOWING
⋘If you should ask me what restraint you should exercise in this work of contemplation, I would answer, 'None whatever!' In all other matters you are bound to use restraint; for example, in the question of food and drink, sleeping, keeping warm or cool, in long prayers or time spent reading, or in conversation with fellow Christians. In all this you get the right balance. But in contemplation, be abandoned! I want you never to cease from this work as long as you live.

I am not saying that you can continue in it always with the same freshness; that cannot be. Illness or some other disorder of body or soul, or physical needs will greatly hinder you in contemplation, and pull you down. But you should always attend to your work in intention if not in actuality: there is no 'time off'! So, for the love of God, take care of yourself and try not to fall ill. Don't let illness be the cause of weakness on your part. I tell

you honestly, contemplation demands great tranquillity, whole-
ness, and purity in both body and soul.

So, for the love of God, discipline your body and soul alike,
keeping fit and healthy. If you should get ill, through circumstances beyond your control, bear it patiently and wait patiently
upon God's mercy. That is all you need do. It is true to say that
patience in sickness and other forms of trouble pleases God much
more than any splendid devotion that you might show in health.

The cloud of unknowing

THE CLOUD OF UNKNOWING

ᥫFor at the first time when ... thou findest but a darkness, and
as it were a cloud of unknowing, thou knowest not what, saying
that thou feelest in thy will a naked intent unto God. This
darkness and this cloud is, howsoever thou dost, between thee
and thy God, and telleth thee that thou mayest not see him
clearly by light of understanding in thy reason, nor feel him in
sweetness of love in thine affection. And therefore shape thee to
bide in this darkness as long as thou mayest, evermore crying after
him that thou lovest. For if ever thou shalt feel him or see him,
as it may be here, it behoveth always to be in this cloud in this
darkness. And if thou wilt busily travail as I bid thee, I trust in his
mercy that thou shalt not come thereto.

Then will he sometimes peradventure send out a beam of
spiritual light, piercing this cloud of unknowing that is between
thee and him; and show thee some of his secrets, about which
man cannot speak. Then shalt thou feel thine affection inflamed
with the fire of his love, far more than I can tell thee, or may or
will at this time. For of that work that falleth only to God, dare I
not take upon me to speak with my blabbering human tongue.

When God seems absent

THE CLOUD OF UNKNOWING

Yet when he [Jesus] heard that Lazarus was sick, he stayed where he was two more days (John 11:6)

✑Whenever the feeling of grace is withdrawn, pride is always the cause; perhaps not actual pride but potential pride, which would have arisen had not the feeling been withdrawn.

Because of this there are some silly young people who think that God is their enemy, when really he is their best friend. Sometimes it is withdrawn because of their carelessness. When this is the case, they experience a deep bitterness which eats into them. Sometimes our Lord deliberately delays the feeling of grace, because in so doing he wishes to make it grow and be more treasured, like a precious thing lost and rediscovered. One of the surest and most important ways by which a soul may know if he is called to contemplation (after such a period of long inability to contemplate) is that it returns suddenly, independently of him, and he has a burning and deep passion to do this work as never before. Often, I think, his joy at its recovery is far greater than his distress at its loss! If this is the case, then it is unmistakably a true sign that he has been called by God to become a contemplative, irrespective of his former or present state.

For it is not what you are or have been that God looks upon with merciful eyes, but what you long to be. St Gregory says that 'all holy desires grow by delays; if they fade by these delays they were never holy desires'. If a man feels increasingly less joy at new discoveries and at the upsurge of his old, deliberate, desire for good, then those passions were never holy. St Augustine speaks of these holy desires saying that 'the life of a good Christian consists of nothing else but holy desire'.

The Perfect cannot be apprehended

THEOLOGIA GERMANICA
[This work was discovered and published in 1516 by Martin Luther, who said of it, 'Next to the Bible and St Augustine, no book has ever come into my hands from which I have learnt more of God and Christ, and man and all things that are.']

Of that which is perfect and that which is in part, and how that which is in part is done away, when that which is perfect is come
୶St Paul saith, 'When that which is perfect is come, then that which is in part shall be done away' (1 Corinthians 13:10). Now mark what is 'that which is perfect', and 'that which is in part'.

'That which is perfect' is a Being, who hath comprehended and included all things in Himself and His own Substance, and without whom, and beside whom, there is no true Substance, and in whom all things have their Substance. For He is the Substance of all things, and is in Himself unchangeable and immoveable, and changeth and moveth all things else. But 'that which is in part', or the Imperfect, is that which hath its source in, or springeth from the Perfect; just as a brightness or a visible appearance floweth out from the sun or a candle, and appeareth to be somewhat, this or that. And it is called a creature; and of all these 'things which are in part', none is the Perfect. So also the Perfect is none of the things which are in part.

The things which are in part can be apprehended, known, and expressed; but the Perfect cannot be apprehended, known, or expressed by any creature as creature. Therefore we do not give a name to the Perfect, for it is none of these. The creature as creature cannot know nor apprehend it, name nor conceive it. 'Now when that which is Perfect is come, then that which is in part shall be done away.' But when doth it come? I say, when as much as may be, it is known, felt and tasted of the soul. For the lack lieth altogether in us, and not in it. In like manner the sun lighteth the whole world, and is as near to one as another, yet a blind man seeth it not; but the fault thereof lieth in the blind man, not in the sun. And like as the sun may not hide its brightness, but must give light unto the earth (for heaven indeed draweth its light and heat from another fountain), so also God, who is the highest Good, willeth not to hide Himself from any, wheresoever He findeth a devout soul, that is thoroughly purified from all creatures. For in what measure we put off the creature, in the same measure are we able to put on the Creator; neither more nor less. For if mine eye is to see anything, it must be single, or else be purified from all other things; and where heat and light enter in, cold and darkness must needs depart; it cannot be otherwise.

But one might say, 'Now since the Perfect cannot be known nor apprehended of any creature, but the soul is a creature, how can it be known by the soul?' Answer: This is why we say, 'by the soul as a creature'. We mean it is impossible to the creature in virtue of its creature-nature and qualities, that by which it saith 'I' and 'myself'. For in whatsoever creature the Perfect shall be known, therein creature-nature, qualities, the I, the Self and the like, must all be lost and done away. This is the meaning of that saying of St Paul: 'When that which is perfect is come' (that is, when it is known), 'then that which is in part' (to wit, creature-nature, qualities, the I, the Self, the Mine) will be despised and counted for nought. So long as we think much of these things, cleave to them with love, joy, pleasure or desire, so long remaineth the Perfect unknown to us. But it might further be said, 'Thou sayest, beside the Perfect there is no Substance, yet sayest again that somewhat floweth out from it: now is not that which hath flowed out from it, something beside it.' Answer: This is why we say, beside it, or without it, there is no true Substance. That which hath flowed forth from it, is no true Substance, and hath no Substance except in the Perfect, but is an accident, or a brightness, or a visible appearance, which is no Substance, and hath no Substance except in the fire whence the brightness flowed forth, such as the sun or a candle.

Humble obedience

THEOLOGIA GERMANICA

How a man shall not seek his own, either in things spiritual or natural but the honour of God only; and how he must enter in by the right door, to wit, by Christ, into eternal life

୬If a man may attain thereunto, to be unto God as his hand is to a man, let him be therewith content, and not seek farther. This is my faithful counsel, and here I take my stand. That is to say, let him strive and wrestle with all his might to obey God and His commandments so thoroughly at all times and in all things, that in him there be nothing, spiritual or natural, which opposeth God; and that his whole soul and body with all their members may stand ready and willing for that to which God hath created them; as ready and willing as his hand is to a man, which is so wholly in his power, that in the twinkling of an eye, he moveth and turneth it whither he will. And when we find it otherwise with us, we must give our whole diligence to amend our state; and this from love and not from fear, and in all things whatsoever, seek and intend the glory and praise of God alone. We must not seek our own, either in things spiritual or in things natural. It must needs be thus, if it is to stand well with us. And every creature oweth this of right and truth unto God, and especially man, to whom, by the ordinance of God, all creatures are made subject, and are servants, that he may be subject to and serve God only.

Further, when a man hath come so far, and climbed so high, that he thinketh and weeneth he standeth sure, let him beware lest the Devil strew ashes and his own bad seed on his heart, and nature seek and take her own comfort, rest, peace, and delight in the prosperity of his soul, and he fall into a foolish, lawless freedom and licentiousness, which is altogether alien to, and at war with, a true life in God. And this will happen to that man who hath not entered, or refuseth to enter in by the right Way and the right Door (which is Christ, as we have said), and imagineth that he would or could come by any other way to the highest truth. He may perhaps dream that he hath attained thereunto, but verily he is in error.

And our witness is Christ, who declareth: 'Verily, verily, I say unto you, He that entereth not by the door into the sheepfold, but climbeth up some other way, the same is a thief and a robber' (John 10:1). A thief, for he robbeth God of His honour and glory, which belong to God alone; he taketh them unto himself, and seeketh and purposeth himself. A murderer, for he slayeth his own soul, and taketh away her life, which is God. For as the body liveth by the soul, even so the soul liveth by God. Moreover, he murdereth all those who follow him, by his doctrine and example. For Christ saith: 'I came down from heaven, not to do Mine own will, but the will of Him that sent Me' (John 6:38). And again: 'Why call ye Me Lord, Lord?' (Luke 6:46) as if he would say, it will avail you nothing to Eternal life. And again: 'Not every one that saith unto Me Lord, Lord, shall enter into the Kingdom of Heaven; but he that doeth the will of My Father which is in Heaven' (Matthew 7:21). But He saith also: 'If thou wilt enter into life, keep the commandments' (Matthew 19:17). And what are the commandments? 'To love the Lord thy God with all thy heart, with all thy soul, and with all thy strength, and with all thy mind; and to love thy neighbour as thyself' (Luke 10:27). And in these two commandments all others are briefly comprehended.

There is nothing more precious to God, or more profitable to man, than humble obedience. In His eyes, one good work, wrought from true obedience, is of more value than a hundred thousand, wrought from self-will, contrary to obedience. Therefore he who hath this obedience need not dread Him, for such a man is in the right way, and following after Christ.

That we may thus deny ourselves, and forsake and renounce all things for God's sake, and give up our own wills, and die unto ourselves, and live unto God alone and to His will, may He help us, who gave up His will to His Heavenly Father, Jesus Christ our Lord, to whom be blessing for ever and ever. Amen.

Pleasing God

MARGERY KEMPE, *THE BOOKE OF MARGERY KEMPE*

◉Daughter, you cannot please God better than to think constantly about his love. Our Lord said, 'Ponder your own wickedness and ponder my goodness.'

Daughter, if you wear a hair shirt, fast with just bread and water, and if you said one thousand Our Father's every day, you would not please Me so well as you do when you are in silence, and allow me to speak to your soul.

Daughter, people who can do nothing else, should frequently use their rosary, but this is not the way of perfection. But it is a step along the road towards perfection. I assure you, daughter, that people who fast and do penance long for the best in life; people who give themselves to numerous devotions long for the best in life; people who give alms long for the best in life. I have frequently told you, daughter, that meditating, weeping and contemplation are the best things you can do on earth. Yet, I fear that you do not believe me, because you continue so often with your rosary. Daughter, if you knew how sweet your love is to me, you would never do anything else except love me with all your heart.

She pondered deeply that our Lord became man, suffering terrible pain, for such an unkind creature as her. Then, with many tears, she asked how she might best please him. He answered her soul, 'Ponder your own wickedness and ponder my goodness.'

Humility

THE IMITATION OF CHRIST, ASCRIBED TO THOMAS À KEMPIS

✐Be not troubled about those who are with you or against you, but take care that God be with you in everything you do. Keep your conscience clear and God will protect you, for the malice of man cannot harm one whom God wishes to help. If you know how to suffer in silence, you will undoubtedly experience God's help. He knows when and how to deliver you; therefore, place yourself in His hands, for it is a divine prerogative to help men and free them from all distress.

It is often good for us to have others know our faults and rebuke them, for it gives us greater humility. When a man humbles himself because of his faults, he easily placates those about him and readily appeases those who are angry with him.

It is the humble man whom God protects and liberates; it is the humble whom He loves and consoles. To the humble He turns and upon them bestows great grace, that after their humiliation He may raise them up to glory. He reveals His secrets to the humble, and with kind invitation bids them come to Him. Thus, the humble man enjoys peace in the midst of many vexations, because his trust is in God, not in the world. Hence, you must not think that you have made any progress until you look upon yourself as inferior to all others.

Deny ourselves and imitate Christ through bearing the cross

THE IMITATION OF CHRIST, ASCRIBED TO THOMAS À KEMPIS

The Voice of Christ

๏My child, the more you depart from yourself, the more you will be able to enter into Me. As the giving up of exterior things brings interior peace, so the forsaking of self unites you to God. I will have you learn perfect surrender to My will, without contradiction or complaint.

Follow Me. I am the Way, the Truth, and the Life. Without the Way, there is no going. Without the Truth, there is no knowing. Without the Life, there is no living. I am the Way which you must follow, the Truth which you must believe, the Life for which you must hope. I am the inviolable Way, the infallible Truth, the unending Life. I am the Way that is straight, the supreme Truth, the Life that is true, the blessed, the uncreated Life. If you abide in My Way you shall know the Truth, and the Truth shall make you free, and you shall attain life everlasting.

If you wish to enter into life, keep My commandments. If you will know the truth, believe in Me. If you will be perfect, sell all. If you will be My disciple, deny yourself. If you will possess the blessed life, despise this present life. If you will be exalted in heaven, humble yourself on earth. If you wish to reign with Me, carry the Cross with Me. For only the servants of the Cross find the life of blessedness and of true light.

The Disciple

๏Lord Jesus, because Your way is narrow and despised by the world, grant that I may despise the world and imitate You. For the servant is not greater than his Lord, nor the disciple above the Master. Let Your servant be trained in Your life, for there is my salvation and true holiness. Whatever else I read or hear does not fully refresh or delight me.

The Voice of Christ

∽My child, now that you know these things and have read them all, happy will you be if you do them. He who has My commandments and keeps them, he it is that loves Me. And I will love him and will show Myself to him, and will bring it about that he will sit down with Me in My Father's Kingdom.

The Disciple

∽Lord Jesus, as You have said, so be it, and what You have promised, let it be my lot to win. I have received the cross, from Your hand I have received it. I will carry it, carry it even unto death as You have laid it upon me. Truly, the life of a good religious man is a cross, but it leads to paradise. We have begun — we may not go back, nor may we leave off.

Take courage, brethren, let us go forward together and Jesus will be with us. For Jesus' sake we have taken this cross. For Jesus' sake let us persevere with it. He will be our help as He is also our leader and guide. Behold, our King goes before us and will fight for us. Let us follow like men. Let no man fear any terrors. Let us be prepared to meet death valiantly in battle. Let us not suffer our glory to be blemished by fleeing from the Cross.

Twenty annotations

IGNATIUS OF LOYOLA, *SPIRITUAL EXERCISES*
[Loyola advised that these annotations should be used with his spiritual exercises.]

৩৩*First Annotation*. The first Annotation is that by this name of Spiritual Exercises is meant every way of examining one's conscience, of meditating, of contemplating, of praying vocally and mentally, and of performing other spiritual actions, as will be said later. For as strolling, walking and running are bodily exercises, so every way of preparing and disposing the soul to rid itself of all the disordered tendencies, and, after it is rid, to seek and find the Divine Will as to the management of one's life for the salvation of the soul, is called a Spiritual Exercise.

Second Annotation. The second is that the person who gives to another the way and order in which to meditate or contemplate, ought to relate faithfully the events of such Contemplation or Meditation, going over the Points with only a short or summary development. For, if the person who is making the Contemplation, takes the true groundwork of the narrative, and, discussing and considering for himself, finds something which makes the events a little clearer or brings them a little more home to him – whether this comes through his own reasoning, or because his intellect is enlightened by the Divine power – he will get more spiritual relish and fruit, than if he who is giving the Exercises had much explained and amplified the meaning of the events. For it is not knowing much, but realizing and relishing things interiorly, that contents and satisfies the soul.

Third Annotation. The third: As in all the following Spiritual Exercises, we use acts of the intellect in reasoning, and acts of the will in movements of the feelings: let us remark that, in the acts of the will, when we are speaking vocally or mentally with God our Lord, or with His Saints, greater reverence is required on our part than when we are using the intellect in understanding.

Fourth Annotation. The fourth: The following Exercises are divided into four parts:

First, the consideration and contemplation on the sins;

Second, the life of Christ our Lord up to Palm Sunday inclusively;

Third, the Passion of Christ our Lord;

Fourth, the Resurrection and Ascension, with the three Methods of Prayer.

Though four weeks, to correspond to this division, are spent in the Exercises, it is not to be understood that each Week has, of necessity, seven or eight days. For, as it happens that in the First Week some are slower to find what they seek – namely, contrition, sorrow and tears for their sins – and in the same way some are more diligent than others, and more acted on or tried by different spirits; it is necessary sometimes to shorten the Week, and at other times to lengthen it. The same is true of all the other subsequent Weeks, seeking out the things according to the subject matter. However, the Exercises will be finished in thirty days, a little more or less.

Fifth Annotation. The fifth: It is very helpful to him who is receiving the Exercises to enter into them with great courage and generosity towards his Creator and Lord, offering Him all his will and liberty, that His Divine Majesty may make use of his person and of all he has according to His most Holy Will.

Sixth Annotation. The sixth: When he who is giving the Exercises sees that no spiritual movements, such as consolations or desolations, come to the soul of him who is exercising himself, and that he is not moved by different spirits, he ought to inquire carefully of him about the Exercises, whether he does them at their appointed times, and how. So too of the Additions, whether he observes them with diligence. Let him ask in detail about each of these things.

Seventh Annotation. The seventh: If he who is giving the Exercises sees that he who is receiving them is in desolation and tempted, let him not be hard or dissatisfied with him, but gentle and indulgent, giving him courage and strength for the future, and laying bare to him the wiles of the enemy of human nature, and getting him to prepare and dispose himself for the consolation coming.

Eighth Annotation. The eighth: If he who is giving the Exercises sees that he who is receiving them is in need of instruction about the desolations and wiles of the enemy – and the same of consolations – he may explain to him, as far as he needs them, the Rules of the First and Second Weeks for recognizing different spirits.

Ninth Annotation. The ninth is to notice, when he who is exercising himself is in the Exercises of the First Week, if he is a person who has not been versed in spiritual things, and is tempted grossly and openly – having, for example, suggested to him obstacles to going on in the service of God our Lord, such as labours, shame and fear for the honour of the world – let him who is giving the Exercises not explain to him the Rules of the Second Week for the discernment of spirits. Because, as much as those of the First Week will be helpful, those of the Second will be harmful to him, as being matter too subtle and too high for him to understand.

Tenth Annotation. The tenth: When he who is giving the Exercises perceives that he who is receiving them is assaulted and tempted under the appearance of good, then it is proper to instruct him about the Rules of the Second Week already mentioned. For, ordinarily, the enemy of human nature tempts under the appearance of good rather when the person is exercising himself in the Illuminative Life, which corresponds to the Exercises of the Second Week, and not so much in the Purgative Life, which corresponds to those of the First.

Eleventh Annotation. The eleventh: It is helpful to him who is receiving the Exercises in the First Week, not to know anything of what he is to do in the Second, but so to labour in the First to attain the object he is seeking as if he did not hope to find in the Second any good.

Twelfth Annotation. The twelfth: As he who is receiving the Exercises is to give an hour to each of the five Exercises or Contemplations which will be made every day, he who is giving the Exercises has to warn him carefully to see always that his soul remains content in the consciousness of having been a full hour in the Exercise, and rather more than less. For the enemy is not a little used to try and make one cut short the hour of such contemplation, meditation or prayer.

Thirteenth Annotation. The thirteenth: It is likewise to be remarked that, as, in the time of consolation, it is easy and not irksome to be in contemplation the full hour, so it is very hard in the time of desolation to fill it out. For this reason, the person who is exercising himself, in order to act against the desolation and conquer the temptations, ought always to stay somewhat more than the full hour; so as to accustom himself not only to resist the adversary, but even to overthrow him.

Fourteenth Annotation. The fourteenth: If he who is giving the Exercises sees that he who is receiving them is going on in consolation and with much fervour, he ought to warn him not to make any inconsiderate and hasty promise or vow: and the more light of character he knows him to be, the more he ought to warn and admonish him. For, though one may justly influence another to embrace the religious life, in which he is understood to make vows of obedience, poverty and chastity, and, although a good work done under vow is more meritorious than one done without it, one should carefully consider the circumstances and personal qualities of the individual and how much help or hindrance he is likely to find in fulfilling the thing he would want to promise.

Fifteenth Annotation. The fifteenth: He who is giving the Exercises ought not to influence him who is receiving them more to poverty or to a promise, than to their opposites, nor more to one state or way of life than to another. For though, outside the Exercises, we can lawfully and with merit influence every one who is probably fit to choose continence, virginity, the religious life and all manner of evangelical perfection, still in the Spiritual Exercises, when seeking the Divine Will, it is more fitting and much better, that the Creator and Lord Himself should communicate Himself to His devout soul, inflaming it with His love and praise, and disposing it for the way in which it will be better able to serve Him in future. So, he who is giving the Exercises should not turn or incline to one side or the other, but standing in the centre like a balance, leave the Creator to act immediately with the creature, and the creature with its Creator and Lord.

Sixteenth Annotation. The sixteenth: For this – namely, that the Creator and Lord may work more surely in His creature – it is very expedient, if it happens that the soul is attached or inclined to a thing inordinately, that one should move himself, putting forth all his strength, to come to the contrary of what he is wrongly drawn to. Thus if he inclines to seeking and possessing an office or benefice, not for the honour and glory of God our Lord, nor for the spiritual well-being of souls, but for his own temporal advantage and interests, he ought to excite his feelings to the contrary, being instant in prayers and other spiritual exercises, and asking God our Lord for the contrary, namely, not to want such office or benefice, or any other thing, unless His Divine Majesty, putting his desires in order, change his first inclination for him, so that the motive for desiring or having one thing or another be only the service, honour, and glory of His Divine Majesty.

Seventeenth Annotation. The seventeenth: It is very helpful that he who is giving the Exercises, without wanting to ask or know from him who is receiving them his personal thoughts or sins, should be faithfully informed of the various movements and thoughts which the different spirits put in him. For, according as is more or less useful for him, he can give him some spiritual Exercises suited and adapted to the need of such a soul so acted upon.

Eighteenth Annotation. The eighteenth: The Spiritual Exercises have to be adapted to the dispositions of the persons who wish to receive them, that is, to their age, education or ability, in order not to give to one who is uneducated or of little intelligence things he cannot easily bear and profit by.

Again, that should be given to each one by which, according to his wish to dispose himself, he may be better able to help himself and to profit.

So, to him who wants help to be instructed and to come to a certain degree of contentment of soul, can be given the Particular Examination, and then the General Examination; also, for a half-hour in the morning, the Method of Prayer on the Commandments, the Deadly Sins, etc. Let him be recommended, also, to confess his sins every eight days, and, if he can, to receive the Blessed Sacrament every fifteen days, and better, if he be so moved, every eight. This way is more proper for illiterate or less educated persons. Let each of the Commandments be explained to them; and so of the Deadly Sins, Precepts of the Church, Five Senses, and Works of Mercy.

So, too, should he who is giving the Exercises observe that he who is receiving them has little ability or little natural capacity, from whom not much fruit is to be hoped, it is more expedient to give him some of these easy Exercises, until he confesses his sins. Then let him be given some Examinations of Conscience and some method for going to Confession oftener than was his custom, in order to preserve what he has gained, but let him not go on into the matter of the Election, or into any other Exercises that are outside the First Week, especially when more progress can be made in other persons and there is not time for every thing.

Nineteenth Annotation. The nineteenth: A person of education or ability who is taken up with public affairs or suitable business, may take an hour and a half daily to exercise himself.

Let the end for which man is created be explained to him, and he can also be given for the space of a half-hour the Particular Examination and then the General and the way to confess and to receive the Blessed Sacrament. Let him, during three days every morning, for the space of an hour, make the meditation on the First, Second and Third Sins; then, three other days at the same hour, the meditation on the statement of Sins; then, for three other days at the same hour, on the punishments corresponding to Sins. Let him be given in all three meditations the ten Additions.

For the mysteries of Christ our Lord, let the same course be kept, as is explained below and in full in the Exercises themselves.

Twentieth Annotation. The twentieth: To him who is more disengaged, and who desires to get all the profit he can, let all the Spiritual Exercises be given in the order in which they follow.

In these he will, ordinarily, more benefit himself, the more he separates himself from all friends and acquaintances and from all earthly care, as by changing from the house where he was dwelling, and taking another house or room to live in, in as much privacy as he can, so that it be in his power to go each day to Mass and to Vespers, without fear that his acquaintances will put obstacles in his way.

Mother Church

JOHN CALVIN, *THE INSTITUTES OF CHRISTIAN RELIGION*

৵But as it is now our purpose to discourse of the visible Church, let us learn, from her single title of Mother, how useful, nay, how necessary the knowledge of her is, since there is no other means of entering into life unless she conceive us in the womb and give us birth, unless she nourish us at her breasts, and, in short, keep us under her charge and government, until, divested of mortal flesh, we become like the angels (Matthew 22:30). For our weakness does not permit us to leave the school until we have spent our whole lives as scholars. Moreover, beyond the pale of the Church no forgiveness of sins, no salvation, can be hoped for, as Isaiah and Joel testify (Isaiah 37:32; Joel 2:32). To their testimony Ezekiel subscribes, when he declares, 'They shall not be in the assembly of my people, neither shall they be written in the writing of the house of Israel' (Ezekiel 3:9); as, on the other hand, those who turn to the cultivation of true piety are said to inscribe their names among the citizens of Jerusalem. For which reason it is said in the psalm, 'Remember me, O Lord, with the favour that thou bearest unto thy people: O visit me with thy salvation; that I may see the good of thy chosen, that I may rejoice in the gladness of thy nation, that I may glory with thine inheritance' (Psalm 106:4, 5). By these words the paternal favour of God and the special evidence of spiritual life are confined to his peculiar people, and hence the abandonment of the Church is always fatal.

Scripture shows us God

JOHN CALVIN, *THE INSTITUTES OF CHRISTIAN RELIGION*
୧୭Therefore, though the effulgence which is presented to every eye, both in the heavens and on the earth, leaves the ingratitude of man without excuse, since God, in order to bring the whole human race under the same condemnation, holds forth to all, without exception, a mirror of his Deity in his works, another and better help must be given to guide us properly to God as a Creator. Not in vain, therefore, has he added the light of his Word in order that he might make himself known unto salvation, and bestowed the privilege on those whom he was pleased to bring into nearer and more familiar relation to himself. For, seeing how the minds of men were carried to and fro, and found no certain resting-place, he chose the Jews for a peculiar people, and then hedged them in that they might not, like others, go astray. And not in vain does he, by the same means, retain us in his knowledge, since but for this, even those who, in comparison of others, seem to stand strong, would quickly fall away. For as the aged, or those whose sight is defective, when any book however fair, is set before them, though they perceive that there is something written are scarcely able to make out two consecutive words, but, when aided by glasses, begin to read distinctly, so Scripture, gathering together the impressions of Deity, which, till then, lay confused in our minds, dissipates the darkness, and shows us the true God clearly. God therefore bestows a gift of singular value, when, for the instruction of the Church, he employs not dumb teachers merely, but opens his own sacred mouth; when he not only proclaims that some God must be worshipped, but at the same time declares that He is the God to whom worship is due; when he not only teaches his elect to have respect to God, but manifests himself as the God to whom this respect should be paid…

For if we reflect how prone the human mind is to lapse into forgetfulness of God, how readily inclined to every kind of error, how bent every now and then on devising new and fictitious religions, it will be easy to understand how necessary it was to make such a depository of doctrine as would secure it from either perishing by the neglect, vanishing away amid the errors, or being corrupted by the presumptuous audacity of men. It being thus manifest that God, foreseeing the inefficiency of his image imprinted on the fair form of the universe, has given the assistance of his Word to all whom he has ever been pleased to instruct effectually, we, too, must pursue this straight path, if we aspire in earnest to a genuine contemplation of God; – we must go, I say, to the Word, where the character of God, drawn from his works is described accurately and to the life; these works being estimated, not by our depraved Judgement, but by the standard of eternal truth. If, as I lately said, we turn aside from it, how great soever the speed with which we move, we shall never reach the goal, because we are off the course. We should consider that the brightness of the Divine countenance, which even an apostle declares to be inaccessible (1 Timothy 6:16), is a kind of labyrinth, – a labyrinth to us inextricable, if the Word do not serve us as a thread to guide our path; and that it is better to limp in the way, than run with the greatest swiftness out of it. Hence the Psalmist, after repeatedly declaring (Psalms 93, 96, 97, 99, etc.) that superstition should be banished from the world in order that pure religion may flourish, introduces God as *reigning*; meaning by the term, not the power which he possesses and which he exerts in the government of universal nature, but the doctrine by which he maintains his due supremacy: because error never can be eradicated from the heart of man until the true knowledge of God has been implanted in it.

Let nothing disturb you

TERESA OF AVILA, FROM A BOOKMARK

Let nothing disturb you
nothing frighten you,
all things are passing;
patient endurance
attains all things.
One whom God possesses
lacks nothing,
for God alone suffices.

Our delightful castle

TERESA OF AVILA, _THE INTERIOR CASTLE_

∽Now let us return to our beautiful and delightful castle and see how we can enter it. I seem rather to be talking nonsense, for, if this castle is the soul, there can clearly be no question of our entering it. For we ourselves are the castle: and it would be absurd to tell someone to enter a room when he was in it already! But you must understand that there are many ways of 'being' in a place. Many souls remain in the outer court of the castle, which is the place occupied by the guards; they are not interested in entering it, and have no idea what there is in that wonderful place, or who dwells in it, or even how many rooms it has. You will have read certain books on prayer which advise the soul to enter within itself: and that is exactly what this means.

A short time ago I was told by a very learned man that souls without prayer are like people whose bodies or limbs are paralysed: they possess feet and hands but they cannot control them.

In the same way, there are souls so infirm and so accustomed to busying themselves with outside affairs that nothing can be done for them, and it seems as though they are incapable of entering within themselves at all. So accustomed have they grown to living all the time with the reptiles and other creatures to be found in the outer court of the castle that they have almost become like them; and although by nature they are so richly endowed as to have the power of holding converse with none other than God Himself, there is nothing that can be done for them. Unless they strive to realize their miserable condition and to remedy it, they will be turned into pillars of salt for not looking within themselves, just as Lot's wife was because she looked back.

As far as I can understand, the door of entry into this castle is prayer and meditation: I do not say mental prayer rather than vocal, for, if it is prayer at all, it must be accompanied by meditation. If a person does not think Whom he is addressing, and what he is asking for, and who it is that is asking and of Whom he is asking it, I do not consider that he is praying at all even though he be constantly moving his lips. True, it is sometimes possible to pray without paying heed to these things, but that is only because they have been thought about previously; if a man is in the habit of speaking to God's Majesty as he would speak to his slave, and never wonders if he is expressing himself properly, but merely utters the words that come to his lips because he has learned them by heart through constant repetition, I do not call that prayer at all – and God grant no Christian may ever speak to Him so! At any rate, sisters, I hope in God that none of you will, for we are accustomed here to talk about interior matters, and that is a good way of keeping oneself from falling into such animal-like habits.

Let us say no more, then, of these paralysed souls, who, unless the Lord Himself comes and commands them to rise, are like the man who had lain beside the pool for thirty years: they are unfortunate creatures and live in great peril. Let us rather think of certain other souls, who do eventually enter the castle. These are very much absorbed in worldly affairs; but their desires are good; sometimes, though infrequently, they commend themselves to Our Lord; and they think about the state of their souls, though not very carefully. Full of a thousand preoccupations as they are, they pray only a few times a month, and as a rule they are thinking all the time of their preoccupations, for they are very much attached to them, and, where their treasure is, there is their heart also. From time to time, however, they shake their minds free of them and it is a great thing that they should know themselves well enough to realize that they are not going the right way to reach the castle door. Eventually they enter the first rooms on the lowest floor, but so many reptiles get in with them that they are unable to appreciate the beauty of the castle or to find any peace within it. Still, they have done a good deal by entering at all.

The prayer of union

TERESA OF AVILA, *THE INTERIOR CASTLE*

൫In the prayer of union our souls are deeply asleep to the things of this world and to ourselves. In fact, for the brief period this state lasts, the soul is without consciousness, and without power to think even if it wanted to. At last, there is no need for the soul to struggle to stop thinking. Even if it loves, it cannot understand how or what it is that it loves, nor what it desires. In fact, it has completely died to the world so that it may live more completely to God.

This is a delicious death. It is a withdrawing from all bodily activity; it is a death full of delight, for truly the soul appears to have left the body in order to draw near to God. I don't even know if the body still has life enough in it to breathe. On reflection, I believe it has not; or at least if it does breathe, then it does so without realizing it.

Now the mind wishes to bend all its powers to understanding what is happening – but it does not have the strength. It is so astounded that even if consciousness is not completely lost, no movement is possible. In this state a person may be compared to someone who has fallen into a dead faint.

So let us now turn, to this sign that proves whether or not the prayer of union has been genuinely with God. As you have seen, God has made the soul look utterly foolish, in order that he may more clearly imprint his true wisdom on it. It loses all its senses; it cannot see, hear, or understand anything while this state lasts. It is always a short time, and to the soul may appear even shorter than it really is, but while it lasts God impresses himself within the soul in a way that removes all doubt. When the soul returns to itself it is absolutely certain that it dwelt in God, and God in it. That truth is so firmly fixed that though years may pass before this favour recurs, the soul can never forget it or doubt it. This certainty within the soul is the significant point.

But now you will ask me: how can someone incapable of seeing or understanding anything, see and understand these things? I'm not saying she realizes it at the time, but that when it is over she clearly sees it, not because of a vision but because of a certainty which stays within the soul and which can only have been put there by God. I know of someone who had not learned that God is in all things by presence, power and essence, but then God granted her a favour of this kind which firmly convinced her. She was so sure that although one of those half-learned priests of whom I spoke, and whom she asked in what way God was in us, replied that he was only present in us by grace, she did not believe him. The priest was as ignorant on the subject as she had been before our Lord revealed the truth to her. She questioned other spiritual people on this matter and to her joy they confirmed the truth of her understanding.

You may well ask: if we do not see anything, how can we become so convinced of something? I don't know. It is the work of God. But I do know I'm speaking the truth. If the experience leaves anyone in doubt, I can only say it was not complete union of the soul with God, but union of one of the faculties, or it was one of the many favours which God grants the soul.

The deity penetrates the soul in dark contemplation

JOHN OF THE CROSS, *THE DARK NIGHT OF THE SOUL*

ↂ This dark contemplation is described as 'secret'. Mystical theology has been called secret wisdom by theologians. St Thomas says that this comes into the soul by means of love. The soul's understanding and other faculties are unaware of this because it happens secretly and in darkness. The soul receives it by means of the Holy Spirit and the soul's faculties do not acquire it. The Bride in the Song of Songs correctly says that this happens without the soul's knowledge or understanding and that is why it is called a secret. In addition to the soul's not understanding it nobody else understands it, not even the devil himself, for the master who teaches it to the soul lives within it.

This isn't the only reason it is called secret. It is also called secret because of what it does in the soul. It is secret in the darknesses and the distressful time of purification when the soul is purified by this wisdom of love. While this is happening, the soul cannot talk about it and in the same way after the soul has been illumined the soul still remains silent. Apart from not wanting to talk about it, the soul cannot find the words to express such an exquisite spiritual experience. So it would still remain secret and hidden, even if the soul did want to talk about it and find the correct words for this. This inner wisdom is so single-minded and so all-embracing and so spiritual that it doesn't enter the soul's mind in disguise. Therefore the soul's sense and imagination know that it is experiencing something most unusual and delightful but does not know what. It is like somebody who sees something that he has never seen before and like nothing else he has ever seen. Although he may take pleasure in it, he may not be able to give it a name. He would not be able to say what it was no matter how much he tried, even though he had observed it with his senses. How much less would he be able to describe something that he had not received with his senses. One of the characteristics of God's way of communicating is that it is very intimate and spiritual in its relationship to the soul. It goes beyond all the senses which immediately stand before it in silence.

On patience

FRANCIS OF SALES, *INTRODUCTION TO THE DEVOUT LIFE*

'Ye have need of patience, that, after ye have done the Will of God, ye might receive the promise,' says Saint Paul; and the Saviour said, 'In your patience possess ye your souls.' The greatest happiness of any one is 'to possess his soul'; and the more perfect our patience, the more fully we do so possess our souls. Call often to mind that our Saviour redeemed us by bearing and suffering, and in like manner we must seek our own salvation amid sufferings and afflictions; bearing insults, contradictions and troubles with all the gentleness we can possibly command. Do not limit your patience to this or that kind of trial, but extend it universally to whatever God may send, or allow to befall you. Some people will only bear patiently with trials which carry their own salve of dignity, such as being wounded in battle, becoming a prisoner of war, being ill-used for the sake of their religion, being impoverished by some strife out of which they came triumphant. Now these persons do not love tribulation, but only the honour which attends it. A really patient servant of God is as ready to bear inglorious troubles as those which are honourable. A brave man can easily bear with contempt, slander and false accusation from an evil world; but to bear such injustice at the hands of good men, of friends and relations, is a great test of patience. I have a greater respect for the gentleness with which the great S. Charles Borromeo long endured the public reproaches which a celebrated preacher of a reformed Order used to pour out upon him, than for all the other attacks he bore with. For, just as the sting of a bee hurts far more than that of a fly, so the injuries or contradictions we endure from good people are much harder to bear than any others. But it is a thing which very often happens, and sometimes two worthy men, who are both highly well-intentioned after their own fashion, annoy and even persecute one another grievously.

Be patient, not only with respect to the main trials which beset you, but also under the accidental and accessory annoyances which arise out of them. We often find people who imagine themselves ready to accept a trial in itself who are impatient of its consequences. We hear one man say, 'I should not mind poverty, were it not that I am unable to bring up my children and receive my friends as handsomely as I desire.' And another says, 'I should not mind, were it not that the world will suppose it is my own fault'; while another would patiently bear to be the subject of slander provided nobody believed it. Others, again, accept one side of a trouble but fret against the rest – as, for instance, believing themselves to be patient under sickness, only fretting against their inability to obtain the best advice, or at the inconvenience they are to their friends. But, dear child, be sure that we must patiently accept, not sickness only, but such sickness as God chooses to send, in the place, among the people, and subject to the circumstances which He ordains; and so with all other troubles. If any trouble comes upon you, use the remedies with which God supplies you. Not to do this is to tempt Him; but having done so, wait whatever result He wills with perfect resignation. If He pleases to let the evil be remedied, thank Him humbly; but if it be His will that the evil grow greater than the remedies, patiently bless His Holy Name.

Follow Saint Gregory's advice: When you are justly blamed for some fault you have committed, humble yourself deeply, and confess that you deserve the blame. If the accusation be false, defend yourself quietly, denying the fact; this is but due respect for truth and your neighbour's edification. But if after you have made your true and legitimate defence you are still accused, do not be troubled, and do not try to press your defence – you have had due respect for truth, have the same now for humility. By acting thus you will not infringe either a due care for your good name, or the affection you are bound to entertain for peace, humility and gentleness of heart.

Complain as little as possible of your wrongs, for as a general rule you may be sure that complaining is sin; the rather that self-love always magnifies our injuries: above all, do not complain to people who are easily angered and excited. If it is needful to complain to someone, either as seeking a remedy for your injury, or in order to soothe your mind, let it be to some calm, gentle spirit, greatly filled with the Love of God; for otherwise, instead of relieving your heart, your confidants will only provoke it to still greater disturbance; instead of taking out the thorn which pricks you, they will drive it further into your foot.

Some people when they are ill, or in trouble, or injured by any one, restrain their complaints, because they think (and that rightly) that to murmur betokens great weakness or a narrow mind; but nevertheless, they exceedingly desire and manoeuvre to make others pity them, desiring to be considered as suffering with patience and courage. Now this is a kind of patience certainly, but it is a spurious patience, which in reality is neither more nor less than a very refined, very subtle form of ambition and vanity. To them we may apply the Apostle's words, 'He hath whereof to glory, but not before God.' A really patient man neither complains nor seeks to be pitied; he will speak simply and truly of his trouble, without exaggerating its weight or bemoaning himself; if others pity him, he will accept their compassion patiently, unless they pity him for some ill he is not enduring, in which case he will say so with meekness, and abide in patience and truthfulness, combatting his grief and not complaining of it.

As to the trials which you will encounter in devotion (and they are certain to arise), bear in mind our dear Lord's words: 'A woman, when she is in travail, hath sorrow, because her hour is come; but as soon as she is delivered of the child, she remembereth no more the anguish, for joy that a child is born into the world.' You, too, have conceived in your soul the most gracious of children, even Jesus Christ, and before He can be brought forth you must inevitably travail with pain; but be of good cheer, for when these pangs are over, you will possess an abiding joy, having brought such a man into the world. And He will be really born for you, when He is perfected in your heart by love, and in your actions by imitating His life.

When you are sick, offer all your pains and weakness to our Dear Lord, and ask Him to unite them to the sufferings which

He bore for you. Obey your physician, and take all medicines, remedies and nourishment, for the Love of God, remembering the vinegar and gall He tasted for love of us; desire your recovery that you may serve Him; do not shrink from languor and weakness out of obedience to Him, and be ready to die if He wills it, to His Glory, and that you may enter into His Presence.

Bear in mind that the bee while making its honey lives upon a bitter food: and in like manner we can never make acts of gentleness and patience, or gather the honey of the truest virtues, better than while eating the bread of bitterness, and enduring hardness. And just as the best honey is that made from thyme, a small and bitter herb, so that virtue which is practised amid bitterness and lowly sorrow is the best of all virtues.

Gaze often inwardly upon Jesus Christ crucified, naked, blasphemed, falsely accused, forsaken, overwhelmed with every possible grief and sorrow, and remember that none of your sufferings can ever be compared to His, either in kind or degree, and that you can never suffer anything for Him worthy to be weighed against what He has borne for you.

Consider the pains which martyrs have endured, and think how even now many people are bearing afflictions beyond all measure greater than yours, and say, 'Of a truth my trouble is comfort, my torments are but roses as compared to those whose life is a continual death, without solace, or aid or consolation, borne down with a weight of grief tenfold greater than mine.'

Luther's three masters

JOSEPH HALL, *MEDITATIONS AND VOWS, DIVINE AND MORAL,*
SERVING FOR DIRECTIONS IN CHRISTIAN AND CIVIL PRACTICE
෴ There is none like to Luther's three masters: Prayer,
Temptation, Meditation. Temptation stirs up holy meditation;
meditation prepares to prayer; and prayer makes profit of
temptation and fetcheth all divine knowledge from heaven. Of
others I may learn the theory of divinity, of these only, the
practice. Other masters teach me, by rote, to speak, parrot-like of
heavenly things; these alone, with feeling and understanding.

Reason and the heart

BLAISE PASCAL, *PENSÉES*
෴ We know truth, not only by the reason, but also by the heart,
and it is in this last way that we know first principles; and reason,
which has no part in it, tries in vain to impugn them. The
sceptics, who have only this for their object, labour to no
purpose. We know that we do not dream, and, however
impossible it is for us to prove it by reason, this inability
demonstrates only the weakness of our reason, but not, as they
affirm, the uncertainty of all our knowledge. For the knowledge
of first principles, as space, time, motion, number, is as sure as any
of those which we get from reasoning. And reason must trust
these intuitions of the heart, and must base on them every
argument. (We have intuitive knowledge of the tri-dimensional
nature of space and of the infinity of number, and reason then
shows that there are no two square numbers one of which is
double of the other. Principles are intuited, propositions are
inferred, all with certainty, though in different ways.) And it is as

useless and absurd for reason to demand from the heart proofs of her first principles, before admitting them, as it would be for the heart to demand from reason an intuition of all demonstrated propositions before accepting them.

This inability ought, then, to serve only to humble reason, which would judge all, but not to impugn our certainty, as if only reason were capable of instructing us. Would to God, on the contrary, that we had never need of it, and that we knew everything by instinct and intuition! But nature has refused us this boon. On the contrary, she has given us but very little knowledge of this kind; and all the rest can be acquired only by reasoning.

Therefore, those to whom God has imparted religion by intuition are very fortunate and justly convinced. But to those who do not have it, we can give it only by reasoning, waiting for God to give them spiritual insight, without which faith is only human and useless for salvation.

Prayer is

JEREMY TAYLOR, *HOLY LIVING*

❧Prayer is the ascent of the mind to God. It is an abstract and summary of Christian religion. Prayer is an act of religion and divine worship, confessing His power and His mercy; it celebrates His attributes, and confesses His glories, and reveres His Person, and implores His aid, and gives thanks for His blessings; it is an act of humility, condescension, and dependence, expressed in the prostration of our bodies and humiliation of our spirits; it is an act of charity, when we pray for others; it is an act of repentance, when it confesses and begs pardon for our sins, and exercises every grace according to the design of the man, and the matter of the prayer.

Twelve signs of grace and predestination

JEREMY TAYLOR, *HOLY LIVING*

৬৯That man does certainly belong to God who believes and is baptized into all the articles of the Christian faith

and studies to improve his knowledge in the matters of God, so as may best make him to live a holy life;

he that, in obedience to Christ, worships God diligently, frequently, and constantly, with natural religion, that is of prayer, praises, and thanksgiving;

he that takes all opportunities to remember Christ's death by a frequent sacrament, as it can be had, or else by inward acts of understanding, will, and memory (which is the spiritual communion) supplies the want of the external rite;

he that lives chastely; and is merciful;

and despises the world, using it as a man, but never suffering it to rifle [to effect strongly or injuriously] a duty;

and is just in his dealing, and diligent in his calling;

he that is humble in his spirit;

and obedient to government;

and content in his fortune and employment;

he that does his duty because he loves God;

and especially if after all this he be afflicted, and patient, or prepared to suffer affliction for the cause of God;

the man that hath these twelve signs of grace and predestination does as certainly belong to God, and is His son as surely, as he is His creature.

The throne of delights

THOMAS TRAHERNE, *CENTURIES*

❧Above everything else, our Saviour's cross is the throne of delights. That centre of eternity, that Tree of Life in the middle of God's paradise. There we are entertained with the wonder of the ages. There we enter into the heart of the universe.

'When I am lifted up,' says the Son of Man, 'I will draw all men unto me.' But by what cords? The cords of a man, the cords of love. The cross is the abyss of wonders, the centre of desires, the school of virtues, the house of wisdom, the throne of love, the theatre of joys, and the place of sorrows; it is the root of happiness and the gate of heaven. It is the ensign lifted up for all nations.

There we may see God's goodness, wisdom, and power displayed. There we may see man's sin and infinite value. It is a well of life beneath, in which we may see the face of heaven above: and the only mirror in which all things appear in their proper colours; that is, sprinkled in the blood of our Lord and Saviour. That cross is a tree set on fire with invisible flame, that illuminates all the world. The flame is love: the love in his heart who died on it.

Assurance of God's love

RICHARD BAXTER, *THE SAINTS' EVERLASTING REST*

❧Here is the heaven of heaven! This is the saint's fruition of God; it consists in these sweet, mutual, constant actions and embracings of love. To love, and to be loved: these are the everlasting arms that are underneath (Deuteronomy 33:27). His left hand is under their heads, and with his right hand doth he embrace them (Song of Songs 2:6).

Reader, stop here and think a moment what a state this is. Is it a small thing in your eyes to be loved by God – to be the son, the spouse, the love, the delight of the King of glory? Christian, believe this, and think about it: you will be eternally embraced in the arms of the love which was from everlasting, and will extend to everlasting – of the love which brought the Son of God's love from heaven to earth, from earth to the cross, from the cross to the grave, from the grave to glory – that love which was weary, hungry, tempted, scorned, scourged, buffeted, spat upon, crucified, pierced – which fasted, prayed, taught, healed, wept, sweated, bled, died. That love will eternally embrace you.

When perfect, created love and most perfect, uncreated love meet together, what a blessed meeting it will be!

The time of prayer

BROTHER LAWRENCE, *THE PRACTICE OF THE PRESENCE OF GOD*
⋙ As Brother Lawrence had found such an advantage in walking in the presence of God, it was natural for him to recommend it earnestly to others; but his example was a stronger inducement than any arguments he could propose. His very countenance was edifying; such a sweet and calm devotion appearing in it, as could not but affect the beholders. And it was observed, that in the greatest hurry of business in the kitchen, he still preserved his recollection and heavenly-mindedness. He was never hasty nor loitering, but did each thing in its season, with an even uninterrupted composure and tranquillity of spirit. 'The time of business,' said he, 'does not with me differ from the time of prayer; and in the noise and clutter of my kitchen, while several persons are at the same time calling for different things, I possess God in as great tranquillity as if I were upon my knees at the Blessed Sacrament.'

The love of God

FRANÇOIS FÉNELON, *CHRISTIAN PERFECTION*

꧁Of the love of God, there are various kinds. At least, there are various feelings which go under that name.

First, there is what may be called mercenary or selfish love; that is, that love of God which originates in a sole regard to our own happiness. Those who love God with no other love than this, love Him just as the miser his money, and the voluptuous man his pleasures; attaching no value to God, except as a means to an end; and that end is the gratification of themselves. Such love, if it can be called by that name, is unworthy of God. He does not ask it; He will not receive it. In the language of Francis de Sales, 'it is sacrilegious and impious'.

Second, another kind of love does not exclude a regard to our own happiness as a motive of love, but requires this motive to be subordinate to a much higher one, namely, that of a regard to God's glory. It is a mixed state, in which we regard ourselves and God at the same time. This love is not necessarily selfish and wrong. On the contrary, when the two objects of it, God and ourselves, are relatively in the right position, that is to say, when we love God as He ought to be loved, and love ourselves no more than we ought to be loved, it is a love which, in being properly subordinated, is unselfish and is right.

Of the subjects of this mixed love all are not equally advanced.

Mixed love becomes pure love, when the love of self is relatively, though not absolutely, lost in a regard to the will of God. This is always the case, when the two objects are loved in their due proportion. So that pure love is mixed love when it is combined rightly.

Pure love is not inconsistent with mixed love, but is mixed love carried to its true result. When this result is attained, the motive of God's glory so expands itself, and so fills the mind, that the other motive, that of our own happiness, becomes so small, and so recedes from our inward notice, as to be practically annihilated. It is then that God becomes what He ever ought to be – the centre of the soul, to which all its affections tend; the great moral sun of the soul, from which all its light and all its warmth proceed. It is then that a man thinks no more of himself. He has become the man of a 'single eye'. His own happiness, and all that regards himself, is entirely lost sight of in his simple and fixed look to God's will and God's glory.

We lay ourselves at His feet. Self is known no more; not because it is wrong to regard and to desire our own good, but because the object of desire is withdrawn from our notice. When the sun shines, the stars disappear. When God is in the soul who can think of himself? So that we love God, and God alone; and all other things in and for God.

Caring

FRANÇOIS FÉNELON, *CHRISTIAN PERFECTION*
◡◉Those in the highest state of religious experience desire nothing, except that God may be glorified in them by the accomplishment of His holy will. Nor is it inconsistent with this, that holy souls possess that natural love which exists in the form of love for themselves. Their natural love, however, which, within its proper degree, is innocent love, is so absorbed in the love of God, that it ceases, for the most part, to be a distinct object of consciousness; and practically and truly they may be said to love themselves IN and FOR God. Adam, in his state of innocence, loved himself, considered as the reflex image of God and for God's sake. So that we may either say, that he loved God in

himself, or that he loved himself IN and FOR God. And it is because holy souls, extending their affections beyond their own limit, love their neighbour on the same principle of loving, namely, IN and FOR God, that they may be said to love their neighbours as themselves.

It does not follow, because the love of ourselves is lost in the love of God, that we are to take no care, and to exercise no watch over ourselves. No man will be so seriously and constantly watchful over himself as he who loves himself IN and FOR God alone. Having the image of God in himself, he has a motive strong, we might perhaps say, as that which controls the actions of angels, to guard and protect it.

It may be thought, perhaps, that this is inconsistent with the principle in the doctrines of holy living, which requires in the highest stages of inward experience, to avoid those reflex acts which consist in self-inspection, because such acts have a tendency to turn the mind off from God. The apparent difficulty is reconciled in this way. The holy soul is a soul with God; moving as God moves; doing as God does; looking as God looks. If, therefore, God is looking within us, as we may generally learn from the intimations of His providences, then it is a sign that we are to look within ourselves. Our little eye, our small and almost imperceptible ray, must look in, in the midst of the light of His great and burning eye. It is thus that we may inspect ourselves without a separation from God.

On the same principle, we may be watchful and careful over our neighbours; watching them, not in our own time, but in God's time; not in the censoriousness of nature, but in the kindness and forbearance of grace; not as separate from God, but in concurrence with Him.

'Get rid of all care with regard to your temporal concerns'

PHILIP DODDRIDGE, *THE RISE AND PROGRESS OF RELIGION IN THE SOUL*

⊷I would advise, then, in the first place, 'that as soon as possible, you would endeavour to get rid of all further care with regard to your temporal concerns, by settling them in time, in as reasonable and Christian a manner as you can'. I could wish there may be nothing of that kind to hurry your mind when you are least able to bear it, or to distress or divide those who come after you. Do that which in the presence of God you judge most equitable, and which you verily believe will be most pleasing to him. Do it in as prudent and effectual a manner as you can; and then consider the world as a place you have quite done with, and its affairs as nothing further to you, more than to one actually dead, unless as you may do any good to its inhabitants while yet you continue among them, and may by any circumstance in your last actions or words in life, leave a blessing behind you to those who have been your friends and fellow-travellers, while you have been despatching that journey through it which you are now finishing.

That you may be the more at leisure, and the better prepared for this, 'enter into some serious review of your own state, and endeavour to put your soul into as fit a posture as possible for your solemn appearance before God'. For a solemn thing indeed it is, to go into his immediate presence; to stand before him, not as a supplicant at the throne of his grace, but at his bar as a separate spirit, whose time of probation is over, and whose eternal state is to be immediately determined. Renew your humiliation before God for the imperfections of your life, though it has, in the main, been devoted to his service. Renew your application to the mercies of God as promised in the covenant of grace, and to the blood of Christ as the blessed channel in which they flow. Resign yourself entirely to the divine disposal and conduct, as willing to serve God, either in this world or the other, as he shall see fit. And sensible of your sinfulness on the one hand, and of the divine wisdom and goodness on the other, summon up all the fortitude of your soul to bear, as well as you can, whatever his afflicting hand may further lay upon you, and to receive the last stroke of it, as one who would maintain the most entire subjection to the great and good Father of spirits.

Whatever you suffer, endeavour to show 'yourself an example of patience'. Let that amiable grace 'have its perfect work'; (James 1:4) and since it has so little more to do, let it close the scene nobly. Let there not be a murmuring word; and that there may not, watch against every repining thought. And when you feel any thing of that kind arising, look by faith upon a dying Saviour, and ask your own heart, 'Was not his cross much more painful than the bed on which I lie? Was not his situation, among bloodthirsty enemies, infinitely more terrible than mine amidst the tenderness and care of so many affectionate friends? Did not the heavy load of my sins press him in a much more overwhelming manner than I am pressed by the load of these afflictions ? And yet he bore all, 'as a lamb that is brought to the slaughter' (Isaiah 53:7). Let the remembrance of his sufferings be a means to sweeten yours; yea, let it cause you to rejoice, when you are called to bear the cross for a little while, before you wear the crown. Count it all joy, that you have an opportunity yet once more of honouring God by your patience, which is now acting its last part, and will, in a few days, and perhaps in a few hours, be superseded by complete, everlasting blessedness. And I am willing to hope, that in these views you will not only suppress all passionate complaints, but that your mouth will be filled with the praises of God; and that you will be speaking to those who are about you, not only of his justice, but of his goodness too. So that you will be enabled to communicate your inward joys in such a manner as may be a lively and edifying comment upon those words of the Apostle, 'Tribulation worketh patience; and patience, experience; and experience, hope; even a hope which maketh not ashamed, while the love of God is shed abroad in our hearts by the Holy Ghost, which is given unto us' (Romans 5: 3–5).

And now, my dear friend, 'now is the time, when it is especially expected from you, that you bear an honourable testimony to religion'. Tell those that are about you, as well as you can (for you will never be able fully to express it), what comfort and support you have found in it. Tell them how it has brightened the darkest circumstances of your life: tell them how it now reconciles you to the near views of death. Your words will carry with them a peculiar weight at such a season: there will be a kind of eloquence, even in the infirmities with which you are struggling, while you give them utterance; and you will be heard with attention, with tenderness, with credit. And therefore, when the time of your departure is at hand, with unaffected freedom breathe out your joy, if you then feel (as I hope you will) a holy joy and delight in God. Breathe out, however, your inward peace and serenity of mind, if you be then peaceful and serene: others will mark it, and be encouraged to tread the steps which lead to so happy an end. Tell them what you feel of the vanity of the world, and they may learn to regard it less. Tell them what you feel of the substantial supports of the Gospel, and they may learn to value it more; for they cannot but know that they must lie down on a dying bed too, and must then need all the relief which the Gospel itself can give them.

And to enforce the conviction the more, 'give a solemn charge to those that are about you, that they spend their lives in the service of God, and govern themselves by the principles of real religion'. You may remember that Joshua and David, and other good men did so, when they perceived that the days drew near in which they should die. And you know not how the admonitions of a dying friend, or (as it may be with respect to some) of a dying parent, may impress those who may have disregarded what you and others may have said to them before. At least, make the trial, and die, labouring to glorify God, to save souls, and generously to sow the seeds of goodness and happiness in a world where you have no more harvest to reap. Perhaps they may spring up in a plentiful crop, when the clods of the valley are covering your body: but if not, God will approve it; and the angels that wait around your bed to receive your departing soul will look upon each other with marks of approbation in their countenance, and own that this is to expire like a Christian, and to make a glorious improvement of mortality.

Wandering thoughts

THOMAS WILSON, *SACRA PRIVATA*

❧The best way to prevent wandering in prayer is not to let the mind wander too much at other times; but to have God always in our minds, in the whole course of our lives. Avoid, as much as may be, multiplicity of business. Neither the innocency nor the goodness of the employment will excuse us, if it possess our hearts when we are praying to God. Make it a law to yourself to meditate before you pray: as also to make certain pauses, to see whether your heart goes along with your lips.

The nature and extent of Christian devotion

WILLIAM LAW, *A SERIOUS CALL TO A DEVOUT AND HOLY LIFE*

ↂDevotion is neither private nor public prayer; but prayers, whether private or public, are particular parts or instances of devotion. Devotion signifies a life given, or devoted, to God.

He, therefore, is the devout man, who lives no longer to his own will, or the way and spirit of the world, but to the sole will of God, who considers God in everything, who serves God in everything, who makes all the parts of his common life parts of piety, by doing everything in the Name of God, and under such rules as are conformable to His glory.

We readily acknowledge, that God alone is to be the rule and measure of our prayers; that in them we are to look wholly unto Him, and act wholly for Him; that we are only to pray in such a manner, for such things, and such ends, as are suitable to His glory.

Now let any one but find out the reason why he is to be thus strictly pious in his prayers, and he will find the same as strong a reason to be as strictly pious in all the other parts of his life. For there is not the least shadow of a reason why we should make God the rule and measure of our prayers; why we should then look wholly unto Him, and pray according to His will; but what equally proves it necessary for us to look wholly unto God, and make Him the rule and measure of all the other actions of our life. For any ways of life, any employment of our talents, whether of our parts, our time, or money, that is not strictly according to the will of God, that is not for such ends as are suitable to His glory, are as great absurdities and failings, as prayers that are not according to the will of God. For there is no other reason why our prayers should be according to the will of God, why they should have nothing in them but what is wise, and holy, and heavenly; there is no other reason for this, but that our lives may be of the same nature, full of the same wisdom, holiness, and heavenly tempers, that we may live unto God in the same spirit that we pray unto Him. Were it not our strict duty to live by reason, to devote all the actions of our lives to God, were it not absolutely necessary to walk before Him in wisdom and holiness and all heavenly conversation, doing everything in His Name, and for His glory, there would be no excellency or wisdom in the most heavenly prayers. Nay, such prayers would be absurdities; they would be like prayers for wings, when it was no part of our duty to fly.

As sure, therefore, as there is any wisdom in praying for the Spirit of God, so sure is it, that we are to make that Spirit the rule of all our actions; as sure as it is our duty to look wholly unto God in our prayers, so sure is it that it is our duty to live wholly unto God in our lives. But we can no more be said to live unto God, unless we live unto Him in all the ordinary actions of our life, unless He be the rule and measure of all our ways, than we can be said to pray unto God, unless our prayers look wholly unto Him. So that unreasonable and absurd ways of life, whether in labour or diversion, whether they consume our time, or our money, are like unreasonable and absurd prayers, and are as truly an offence unto God.

It is for want of knowing, or at least considering this, that we see such a mixture of ridicule in the lives of many people. You see them strict as to some times and places of devotion, but when the service of the Church is over, they are but like those that seldom or never come there. In their way of life, their manner of spending their time and money, in their cares and fears, in their pleasures and indulgences, in their labour and diversions, they are like the rest of the world. This makes the loose part of the world generally make a jest of those that are devout, because they see their devotion goes no farther than their prayers, and that when they are over, they live no more unto God, till the time of prayer returns again; but live by the same humour and fancy, and in as full an enjoyment of all the follies of life as other people. This is the reason why they are the jest and scorn of careless and worldly people; not because they are really devoted to God, but because they appear to have no other devotion but that of occasional prayers.

Christian Perfection

JOHN WESLEY, A PLAIN MAN'S GUIDE TO CHRISTIAN HOLINESS

~ Question: What is Christian Perfection?

Answer: The loving God with all our heart, mind, soul, and strength. This implies, that no wrong frame of mind, nothing contrary to love, remains in the soul; and that all the thoughts, words and actions, are governed by pure love.

Q: Do you affirm that this perfection excludes all infirmities, ignorance and mistakes?

A: I continually affirm quite the opposite, and have always done so.

Q: But how can every thought, word and work, be governed by pure love, and the man be subject at the same time to ignorance and mistake?

A: I see no contradiction here: 'A man may be filled with pure love, and still be liable to mistake.' Indeed I do not expect to be freed from actual mistakes till this mortal puts on immortality. I believe this to be a natural consequence of the soul's dwelling in flesh and blood. For we cannot now think at all, but by the mediation of those bodily organs which have suffered equally with the rest of our frame. And hence we cannot avoid sometimes thinking wrong, till this corruptible shall have put on incorruption.

Q: If people live without sin, does not this exclude the necessity of a Mediator?

A: Firstly, not only sin, properly so called (that is, a voluntary transgression of a known law), but sin, incorrectly so called (that is, an involuntary transgression of a divine law, known or unknown), needs the atoning blood.

Secondly, I believe there is no such perfection in this life as excludes these involuntary transgressions which I apprehend to be naturally consequent on the ignorance and mistakes inseparable from mortality.

Thirdly, therefore, 'sinless perfection' is a phrase I never use, lest I should seem to contradict myself.

Fourthly, I believe a person filled with love of God is still liable to these involuntary transgressions.

Fifthly, such transgressions you may call sins, if you please: I do not, for these reasons above-mentioned.

Q: How shall we avoid setting perfection too high or too low?

A: By keeping to the Bible, and setting it just as high as the scripture does. It is nothing higher and nothing lower than this – the pure love of God and man; the loving of God with all our heart and soul, and our neighbour as ourselves. It is love governing the heart and life, running through our whole mentality, words, and actions.

Q: Is it proof that a person is not perfect if he is surprised or thrown into confusion by a noise, a fall, or some sudden danger?

A: It is not; for one may jump, tremble, change colour, or be otherwise disordered in body, while the soul is calmly stayed on God, and remains in perfect peace.

Q: Is death to sin, and renewal in love, gradual or instantaneous?

A: A man may be dying for some time; yet he does not, properly speaking, die till the instant the soul is separated from the body; and in that instant he lives the life of eternity. In the same way he may be dying to sin for some time; yet he is not dead to sin, till sin is separated from his soul; and in that instant he lives the full life of love.

Speaking to God

E.B. PUSEY, *TRACTS FOR THE TIMES*

ↄ Put off the hour of prayer for nothing of your own; so as not to make a stroke more with the pen.

Bustle hurts the mind and soul, and benefits nothing.

Have some arrow prayers to pray during the day, or a psalm.

A good watchmaker is one who makes watches and prays: a good housemaid is one who sweeps and prays.

Prayer may be equally with words or without: it may be 'Jesu', 'my God and my all'. Like the Samians throwing their empty sack in front of the Spartans and saying the word 'flour'; which they said was a word too much, since if they only saw the empty sack it was enough; so if we bring our emptiness only before God, he will fill it.

It would be a very good prayer to offer God your whole being, with a full earnest wish to do all to his honour and praise; that is, to seek to please him in everything; and to agree that every time the clock strikes you renew this with great intensity.

Speak to God as a child to One it may freely speak to.

Always choose some special thing to ask for at Holy Communion, and make it your earnest aim afterwards. After Holy Communion, make acts of the mind to recall it. 'Abide with me.'

'Leave me not.' Never mind their being formal at first, till collectedness is gained as a thing of course.

Be thankful for everything: especially for what is against your will.

St Catherine of Siena made a cell in her heart. Afterwards, in a most busy life she could keep quite close to God and without the least distraction.

DREAMS AND VISIONS

❧⟨∞⟩❧

The Dream of the Rood

THE DREAM OF THE ROOD
[This eighth-century poem and meditation on the death of
Christ is presented from the point of view of the rood (or cross)
on which Christ was crucified.]

Hear while I tell about the best of dreams
Which came to me the middle of one night
While humankind were sleeping in their beds.
It was as though I saw a wondrous tree
Towering in the sky suffused with light...
... the best
Of woods began to speak these words to me:
'It was long past — I still remember it —
That I was cut down at the copse's end,
Moved from my roots. Strong enemies there took me,
Told me to hold aloft their criminals,
Made me a spectacle. Men carried me
Upon their shoulders, set me on a hill,

A host of enemies there fastened me.
And then I saw the Lord of all mankind
Hasten with eager zeal that He might mount
Upon me. I durst not against God's word
Bend down or break, when I saw tremble all
The surface of the earth. Although I might
Have struck down all the foes, yet stood I fast.
Then the young hero (who was God almighty)
Got ready, resolute and strong in heart.
He climbed on to the lofty gallows-tree,
Bold in the sight of many watching men,
When he intended to redeem mankind.
I trembled as the warrior embraced me.
But still I dared not bend down to the earth,
Fall to the ground. Upright I had to stand.
A rood I was raised up; and I held high
The noble King, the Lord of heaven above.
I dared not stoop. They pierced me with dark nails;
The scars can still be clearly seen on me,
The open wounds of malice. Yet might I
Not harm them. They reviled us both together.
I was made wet all over with the blood
Which poured out from His side, after He had
Sent forth His spirit. And I underwent
Full many a dire experience on that hill.
I saw the God of hosts stretched grimly out.
Darkness covered the Ruler's corpse with clouds,
His shining beauty; the shadows passed across,
Black in the darkness. All creation wept,
Bewailed the King's death; Christ was on the cross.
And yet I saw men coming from afar,
Hastening to the Prince. I watched it all.'

I alone can satisfy him

CATHERINE OF SIENA, *TREATISE ON DIVINE PROVIDENCE*
[Catherine dictated this while in a state of ecstasy.]

∽◎Man is placed above all creatures, and not beneath them, and he cannot be satisfied or content except in something greater than himself. Greater than himself there is nothing but Myself, the Eternal God. Therefore I alone can satisfy him, and, because he is deprived of this satisfaction by his guilt, he remains in continual torment and pain. Weeping follows pain, and when he begins to weep, the wind strikes the tree of self-love, which he has made the principle of all his being.

God as Sustainer

JULIAN OF NORWICH, *REVELATIONS OF DIVINE LOVE*
∽◎In this Revelation he showed me something else, a tiny thing, no bigger than a hazelnut, lying in the palm of the hand, and as round as a ball. I looked at it, puzzled, and thought, 'What is it?'

The answer came: 'It is everything that is made.'

I wondered how it could survive. It was so small that I expected it to shrivel up and disappear.

Then I was answered, 'It exists now and always because God loves it.' Then I understood that everything exists through the love of God. In this small thing I saw three truths: first God made it, second God loves it, and third God looks after it. But what he really means to me as Maker and Keeper and Lover, I cannot tell.

Jesus our true Mother

JULIAN OF NORWICH, *REVELATIONS OF DIVINE LOVE*

꧁God is as truly our Mother as he is our Father.

Our great Father, almighty God, who is being, knew and loved us before time began. In that knowledge, out of his wonderful deep love, and with the foresight and counsel of the blessed Trinity, he willed that the second person become our Mother.

Our Father willed it, our Mother accomplished it, our good Lord the Holy Spirit established it. So we must love our God in whom we have our being. We must reverently thank and praise him for our creation, fervently ask our Mother for mercy and compassion, and our Lord the Holy Spirit for help and grace.

From nature, mercy and grace – from these three – comes our life. From them we have humility and gentleness and pity. From them, too, we get our hatred of sin and wickedness, for it is in the nature of virtue to hate these.

So Jesus is our true Mother in nature because of our first creation, and he is our true Mother in grace because he took our created nature. In the second person there is all the loving service and sweet spontaneous care that belongs to beloved motherhood, and in him our will for God is always safe, both naturally and by grace, because of his own innate goodness.

I saw that the motherhood of God can be looked at in three ways. The first is his creation of our human nature; the second his assumption of nature – from which stems the motherhood of grace; and the third is the practical outworking of motherhood, as a result of which, and by that same grace, it spreads out in endless height, breadth, length, and depth. And all is one here.

The Crucifixion

JULIAN OF NORWICH, *REVELATIONS OF DIVINE LOVE*

∾As I looked I saw the body bleeding heavily, apparently from the flogging. The smooth skin was gashed and all over his body I saw deep weals in the tender flesh caused by many sharp blows. The blood flowed so hot and thick that neither the wounds nor the skin could be seen: it was all covered in blood. The blood flowed all down his body, but at the point of falling to the ground, it disappeared. The bleeding continued for a while, giving me time to see it and think about it. It was so heavy that I thought that if it had been real the whole bed and everything around would have been soaked in blood.

Then the idea came to me that out of his tender love for us God has created a vast supply of water for us to use to make ourselves comfortable on this earth. Yet he would rather that we make ourselves at home with him by using his holy blood to wash ourselves clean from our sin: for no liquid has been made which he would prefer to give. It is as plentiful as it is precious because it is divine. It is part of us, and is most blissfully ours because of his precious love.

The beloved blood of our Lord Jesus Christ is truly as plentiful as it is precious. Look and see for yourself. It flows over the whole world ready to wash every human being clean from all sin, present, past and future, if they are willing.

I saw his Passion

JULIAN OF NORWICH, *REVELATIONS OF DIVINE LOVE*

∾I saw the red blood trickle down from under the garland of thorns, a stream of hot, fresh blood, just as it was in the time of his Passion when the crown was pressed on to the blessed head of the God-Man who suffered in this way for me. And I saw clearly, powerfully and truly, that it was none other than Jesus himself who showed this vision to me.

In that same vision, the Trinity suddenly filled my heart with the deepest joy, and I knew that all those who go to heaven will experience this joy for ever. For the Trinity is God: God is the Trinity; the Trinity is our Creator and Keeper, the Trinity is our eternal love, joy and bliss, through our Lord Jesus Christ. This was revealed to me in this first vision and indeed in all of them, for it seems to me that wherever Jesus appears the blessed Trinity is also present.

'*Benedicite, Domine!*' ['Welcome, O Lord!'] I cried, and I meant it in all reverence and shouted it at the top of my voice! I was overwhelmed with wonder that he, so holy and awesome, should be so at home with the likes of me – I, who am so sinful, with such a wretched earthly body.

All will be well

JULIAN OF NORWICH, *REVELATIONS OF DIVINE LOVE*

∾All will be well, and all will be well, and all manner of things will be well.

SERMONS AND LECTURES

❧

How merciful is God

EPHRAEM THE SYRIAN, *SERMON ON THE SINFUL WOMAN*
‿Hear and be comforted, beloved, how merciful is God. To the sinful woman He forgave her offences; yea, He upheld her when she was afflicted. With clay He opened the eyes of the blind, so that the eyeballs beheld the light … And to us He has given the pearls; His holy Body and Blood. He brought His medicines secretly; and with them He heals openly. And He wandered round in the land of Judea, like a physician, bearing his medicines. Simon invited Him to the feast, to eat bread in his house. The sinful woman rejoiced when she heard that He sat and was feasting in Simon's house; her thoughts gathered together like the sea, and like the billows her love surged. She beheld the Sea of Grace, how it had forced itself into one place; and she resolved to go and drown all her wickedness in its billows.

She bound her heart, because it had offended, with chains and tears of suffering; and she began weeping: 'What avails me this fornication? What avails this lewdness? I have defiled the innocent ones without shame; I have corrupted the orphan; and without fear I have robbed the merchants of merchandise, and my rapacity was not satisfied ... Why did I not win me one man, who might have corrected my lewdness? For one man is of God, but many are of Satan.'

These things she said secretly; then began to do openly. She took up the gold in her palm, and carried the alabaster box in her hands. Then hastily went she forth in sadness to the perfumer ... 'Take thee the gold,' she said to the perfumer, 'as much as thou demandest, and give me the precious ointment; take thee that which endures not and give me that which endures; and I will go to Him who endures, and will buy that which endures ... A Man has met me today Who bears riches in abundance. He has robbed me and I have robbed Him; He has robbed me of my transgressions and sins, and I have robbed Him of His wealth ... She took up the ointment and went forth. ...

The sinful woman full of transgressions stood clinging by the door. She clasped her arms in prayer, and thus she spake beseeching: 'Blessed Son Who hast descended to earth for the sake of man's redemption, close not Thy door in my face; for Thou hast called me and lo! I come. I know that Thou hast not rejected me; open for me the door of Thy mercy, that I may come in, O my Lord, and find refuge in Thee, from the Evil One and his hosts! I was a sparrow, and the hawk pursued me, and I have fled and taken refuge in Thy nest. I was a heifer, and the yoke galled me, and I will turn back my wanderings to Thee. Lay upon me the shoulder of Thy yoke that I may take it on me, and work with Thy oxen.' Thus did the harlot speak at the door with much weeping. The master of the house looked and saw her, and the colour of his visage was changed; and he began thus to address her, the harlot: 'Depart thou hence, O harlot, for this man who abides in our house is a man that is righteous, and they that are of his companions are blameless. Is it not enough for thee, harlot,

that thou hast corrupted the whole town? Thou hast corrupted
the chaste without shame; thou hast robbed the orphans, and hast
not blushed, and hast plundered the merchants' wares, and thy
countenance is not abashed. From him thou labourest to take his
heart. But from him thy net takes no spoil. For this man is righteous indeed, and they of his company are blameless.'

The sinful woman answered and said to him, even to Simon
when he had ceased: 'Thou surely art the guardian of the door,
O thou that knowest things that are secret; I will propose the
matter in the feast, and thou shall be free from blame. And if there
be any that wills me to come in, he will bid me and I will come
in.' Simon ran and closed the door, and approached and stood afar
off. And he tarried a long time and proposed not the matter in
the feast. But He, Who knows what is secret, beckoned to Simon
and said to him: 'Come hither, Simon, I bid thee; does any one
stand at the door? Whosoever he be, open to him that he may
come in; let him receive what he needs, and go. If he be hungry
and hunger for bread, lo! in thy house is the table of life; and if
he be thirsty, and thirst for water, lo! the blessed fountain is in thy
dwelling. And if he be sick and ask for healing, lo! the great
Physician is in thy house. Suffer sinners to look upon Me, for
their sakes have I abased Myself. I will not ascend to heaven, to
the dwelling whence I came down, until I bear back the sheep
that has wandered from its Father's house, and lift it up on My
shoulders and bear it aloft to heaven.'

Simon answered and thus he said to Jesus, when He had done
speaking: 'My Lord, this woman that stands in the doorway is a
harlot: she is lewd and not free-born, polluted from her childhood. And Thou, my Lord, art a righteous man, and all are eager
to see Thee; and if men see Thee having speech with the harlot,
all men will flee from beside Thee, and no man will salute Thee.'
Jesus answered, and thus He said to Simon when he was done

speaking: 'Whosoever it be, open for him to come in, and thou shall be free from blame; and though his offences be many, without rebuke I bid thee receive him.'

Simon approached and opened the door, and began thus to speak: 'Come, enter, fulfil that thou willest, to him who is even as thou.' The sinful woman, full of transgressions, passed forward and stood by His feet, and clasped her arms in prayer, and with these words she spake: 'Mine eyes have become watercourses that cease not from watering the fields, and today they wash the feet of Him Who follows after sinners. This hair, abundant in locks from my childhood till this day, let it not grieve Thee that it should wipe this holy body. The mouth that has kissed the lewd, forbid it not to kiss the body that remits transgressions and sins.' These things the harlot spake to Jesus, with much weeping. And Simon stood afar off to see what He would do to her. But He Who knows the things that are secret, beckoned to Simon and said to him: 'Lo! I will tell thee, O Simon, what thy meditation is, concerning the harlot. Within thy mind thou imaginest and within thy soul thou saidst, "I have called this man righteous, but lo! the harlot kisses Him. I have called Him to bless my possessions, and lo! the harlot embraces Him." O Simon, there were two debtors, whose creditor was one only; one owed him five-hundred pence, and the other owed fifty. And when the creditor saw that neither of these two had aught, the creditor pardoned and forgave them both their debt. Which of them ought to render the greater thanks? He who was forgiven five hundred, or he who was forgiven fifty?'

Simon answered, and thus he said to Jesus, when He had done speaking: 'He who was forgiven five hundred ought to render the greater thanks.'

Jesus answered and thus He said: 'Thou art he that owes five hundred, and this woman owes fifty. Lo! I came into thy house,

O Simon; and water for My feet thou broughtest not; and this woman, of whom thou saidst that she was an harlot, one from her childhood defiled, has washed My feet with her tears, and with her hair she has wiped them. Ought I to send her away, O Simon, without receiving forgiveness? Verily, verily, I say unto thee, I will write of her in the Gospel. Go, O woman, thy sins are forgiven thee and all thy transgression is covered; henceforth and to the end of the world.'

May our Lord account us worthy of hearing this word of His: 'Come, enter, ye blessed of My Father, inherit the kingdom made ready for all who shall do My will, and observe all My commandments.' To Him be glory; on us be mercy; at all times. Amen! Amen!

Is there anyone who is a devout lover of God?

JOHN CHRYSOSTOM
[The Easter Sermon of John Chrysostom, preached while he was Pastor of Constantinople, in c. 400 AD.]

Is there anyone who is a devout lover of God?
Let them enjoy this beautiful bright festival!
Is there anyone who is a grateful servant?
Let them rejoice and enter into the joy of their Lord!

Are there any weary with fasting?
Let them now receive their wages!
If any have toiled from the first hour,
let them receive their due reward;
If any have come after the third hour,

let him with gratitude join in the Feast!
And he that arrived after the sixth hour,
let him not doubt; for he too shall sustain no loss.
And if any delayed until the ninth hour,
let him not hesitate; but let him come too.
And he who arrived only at the eleventh hour,
let him not be afraid by reason of his delay.

For the Lord is gracious and receives the last even as the first.
He gives rest to him that comes at the eleventh hour,
as well as to him that toiled from the first.
To this one He gives, and upon another He bestows.
He accepts the works as He greets the endeavour.
The deed He honours and the intention He commends.

Let us all enter into the joy of the Lord!
First and last alike receive your reward;
rich and poor, rejoice together!

Sober and slothful, celebrate the day!

You that have kept the fast, and you that have not,
rejoice today for the Table is richly laden!
Feast royally on it, the calf is a fatted one.
Let no one go away hungry. Partake, all, of the cup of faith.
Enjoy all the riches of His goodness!

Let no one grieve at his poverty,
for the universal kingdom has been revealed.
Let no one mourn that he has fallen again and again;
for forgiveness has risen from the grave.

Let no one fear death, for the Death of our Saviour has set us
   free.
He has destroyed it by enduring it.

He destroyed Hades when He descended into it.
He put it into an uproar even as it tasted of His flesh.
Isaiah foretold this when he said,
'You, O Hell, have been troubled by encountering Him below.'

Hell was in an uproar because it was done away with.
It was in an uproar because it is mocked.
It was in an uproar, for it is destroyed.
It is in an uproar, for it is annihilated.
It is in an uproar, for it is now made captive.
Hell took a body, and discovered God.
It took earth, and encountered Heaven.
It took what it saw, and was overcome by what it did not see.
O death, where is thy sting?
O Hades, where is thy victory?

Christ is Risen, and you, O death, are annihilated!
Christ is Risen, and the evil ones are cast down!
Christ is Risen, and the angels rejoice!
Christ is Risen, and life is liberated!
Christ is Risen, and the tomb is emptied of its dead;
for Christ having risen from the dead,
is become the first-fruits of those who have fallen asleep.

To Him be Glory and Power forever and ever. Amen!

'Come unto me, all ye that labour and are heavy laden, and I will give you rest,' (Matthew 11:28)

AUGUSTINE, *SERMONS ON SELECTED LESSONS OF THE NEW TESTAMENT*, SERMON 20

꧁It seems strange to some, Brethren, when they hear the Lord say, 'Come unto Me, all ye that labour and are heavy laden, and I will refresh you. Take my yoke upon you and learn of Me, for I am meek and lowly in heart, and ye shall find rest unto your souls. For My yoke is easy and My burden is light.' And they consider that they who have fearlessly bowed their necks to this yoke, and have with much submission taken this burden upon their shoulders, are tossed about and exercised by so great difficulties in the world, that they seem not to be called from labour to rest, but from rest to labour rather; since the Apostle also saith, 'All who will live godly in Christ Jesus, shall suffer persecution.' So one will say, 'How is the yoke easy, and the burden light,' when to bear this yoke and burden is nothing else, but to live godly in Christ? And how is it said, 'Come unto Me, all ye that labour and are heavy laden, and I will refresh you'? and not rather said, 'Come ye who are at ease and idle, that ye may labour.' For so he found those men idle and at ease, whom he hired into the vineyard, that they might bear the heat of the day. And we hear the Apostle under that easy yoke and light burden say, 'In all things approving ourselves as the ministers of God, in much patience, in afflictions, in necessities, in distresses, in stripes', etc., and in another place of the same Epistle, 'Of the Jews five times received I forty stripes save one. Thrice was I beaten with rods, once was I stoned, thrice have I suffered shipwreck, a night and a day have I been in the deep': and the rest of the perils, which may be enumerated indeed, but endured they cannot be but by the help of the Holy Spirit.

All these grievous and heavy trials which he mentioned, did he very frequently and abundantly sustain; but in very deed the Holy Spirit was with him in the wasting of the outward man, to renew the inner man from day to day, and by the taste of spiritual rest in the affluence of the delights of God to soften down by the hope of future blessedness all present hardships, and to alleviate all heavy trials. Lo, how sweet a yoke of Christ did he bear, and how light a burden; so that he could say that all those hard and grievous sufferings at the recital of which as just above every hearer shudders, were a 'light tribulation'; as he beheld with the inward eyes, the eyes of faith, at how great a price of things temporal must be purchased the life to come, the escape from the everlasting pains of the ungodly, the full enjoyment, free from all anxiety, of the eternal happiness of the righteous. Men suffer themselves to be cut and burnt, that the pains not of eternity, but of some more lasting sore than usual, may be bought off at the price of severer pain. For a languid and uncertain period of a very short repose, and that too at the end of life, the soldier is worn down by all the hard trials of war, restless it may be for more years in his labours, than he will have to enjoy his rest in ease. To what storms and tempests, to what a fearful and tremendous raging of sky and sea, do the busy merchantmen expose themselves, that they may acquire riches inconstant as the wind, and full of perils and tempests, greater even than those by which they were acquired! What heats, and colds, what perils, from horses, from ditches, from precipices, from rivers, from wild beasts, do huntsmen undergo, what pain of hunger and thirst, what straitened allowances of the cheapest and meanest meat and drink, that they may catch a beast! and sometimes after all, the flesh of the beast for which they endure all this is of no use for the table. And although a boar or a stag be caught, it is more sweet to the hunter's mind because it has been caught, than it is to the eater's palate because it is dressed. By what sharp corrections of almost daily stripes is the tender age of boys brought under! By what great pains even of watching and abstinence in the schools are they exercised, not to learn true wisdom, but for the sake of riches, and the honours of an empty show, that they may learn arithmetic, and other literature, and the deceits of eloquence!

Now in all these instances, they who do not love these things feel them as great severities; whereas they who love them endure the same, it is true, but they do not seem to feel them severe. For love makes all, the hardest and most distressing things, altogether easy, and almost nothing. How much more surely then and easily will charity do with a view to true blessedness, that which mere desire does as it can, with a view to what is but misery? How easily is any temporal adversity endured, if it be that eternal punishment may be avoided, and eternal rest procured! Not without good reason did that vessel of election say with exceeding joy, 'The sufferings of this present time are not worthy to be compared with the glory which shall be revealed in us.' See then how it is that that 'yoke is easy, and that burden light.' And if it be strait to the few who choose it, yet is it easy to all who love it. The Psalmist saith, 'Because of the words of Thy lips I have kept hard ways.' But the things which are hard to those who labour, lose their roughness to those same men when they love. Wherefore it has been so arranged by the dispensation of the Divine goodness, that to 'the inner man who is renewed from day to day', placed no longer under the Law but under Grace, and freed from the burdens of numberless observances which were indeed a heavy yoke, but meetly imposed on a stubborn neck, every grievous trouble which that prince who is cast forth could inflict from without on the outward man, should through the easiness of a simple faith, and a good hope, and a holy charity, become light through the joy within. For to a good will nothing is so easy, as this good will to itself, and this is enough for God. How much soever therefore this world may rage, most truly did the angels exclaim when the Lord was born in the flesh, 'Glory to God in the highest, and on earth peace to men of good will'; because 'His yoke', who was then born, 'is easy, and His burden light'. And as the Apostle saith, 'God is faithful, who will not suffer us to be tempted above that we are able to bear; but will with the temptation also make a way to escape, that we may be able to bear it.'

We must all be partakers in Christ's Resurrection life.

LEO I
[This sermon was delivered on Holy Saturday in the vigil of Easter.]

⋘We must all be partakers in Christ's Resurrection life. In my last sermon, dearly-beloved, we explained to you our participation in the cross of Christ, whereby the life of believers contains in itself the mystery of Easter, and thus what is honoured at the feast is celebrated by our practice. And how useful this is you yourselves have proved, and by your devotion have learnt, how your souls and bodies greatly benefit from longer fasts, more frequent prayers, and more liberal alms ... Since, therefore, by our forty days' observance we have wished to bring about this effect, that we should feel something of the Cross at the time of the Lord's Passion, we must strive to be found partakers also of Christ's Resurrection, and 'pass from death unto life', while we are in this body ... We must die, therefore, to the devil and live to God: we must perish to iniquity that we may rise to righteousness. Let the old sink, that the new may rise; and since, as says the Truth, 'no one can serve two masters,' let not him be lord who has caused the overthrow of those that stood, but Him Who has raised the fallen to victory.

God did not leave His soul in hell, nor suffer His flesh to see corruption. Accordingly, since the Apostle says, 'the first man is of the earth earthy, the second man is from heaven heavenly. As is the earthy, such also are they that are earthy; and as is the heavenly, such also are they that are heavenly. As we have borne the image of the earthy, so let us also bear the image of Him Who is from heaven,' we must greatly rejoice over this change, whereby we are translated from earthly degradation to heavenly dignity through His unspeakable mercy. The Saviour's resurrection did not long keep His soul in Hades, nor His flesh in the tomb.

Christ's manifestation after the Resurrection showed that His Person was essentially the same as before. And then there followed many proofs, whereon the authority of the Faith to be preached through the whole world might be based. And although the rolling away of the stone, the empty tomb, the arrangement of the linen cloths, and the angels who narrated the whole deed by themselves fully built up the truth of the Lord's Resurrection, yet did He often appear plainly to the eyes both of the women and of the Apostles not only talking with them, but also remaining and eating with them, and allowing Himself to be handled by the eager and curious hands of those whom doubt assailed. For to this end He entered when the doors were closed upon the disciples, and gave them the Holy Spirit by breathing on them, and after giving them the light of understanding opened the secrets of the Holy Scriptures, and again Himself showed them the wound in the side, the prints of the nails, and all the marks of His most recent Passion, whereby it might be acknowledged that in Him the properties of the Divine and Human Nature remained undivided, and we might in such sort know that the Word was not what the flesh is, as to confess God's only Son to be both Word and Flesh.

Being saved by hope, we must not fulfil the lusts of the flesh. Let us not then be taken up with the appearances of worldly matters, neither let our contemplations be diverted from heavenly to earthly things.

Our godly resolutions must continue all the year round, not be confined to Eastier only. Let God's people then recognize that they are a new creation in Christ, and with all vigilance understand by Whom they have been adopted and Whom they have adopted. Let not the things, which have been made new, return to their ancient instability; and let not him who has 'put his hand to the plough' forsake his work, but rather attend to that which he sows than look back to that which he has left behind. Let no one fall back into that from which he has risen, but, even though from bodily weakness he still languishes under certain maladies, let him urgently desire to be healed and raised up. For this is the path of health through imitation of the Resurrection begun in Christ, whereby, notwithstanding the many accidents and falls to which in this slippery life the traveller is liable, his feet may be guided from the quagmire on to solid ground, for, as it is written, 'the steps of a man are directed by the Lord, and He will delight in his way. When the just man falls he shall not be overthrown, because the Lord will stretch out His hand.' These thoughts, dearly-beloved, must be kept in mind not only for the Easter festival, but also for the sanctification of the whole life, and to this our present exercise ought to be directed, that what has delighted the souls of the faithful by the experience of a short observance may pass into a habit and remain unalterably, and if any fault creep in, it may be destroyed by speedy repentance. And because the cure of old-standing diseases is slow and difficult, remedies should be applied early, when the wounds are fresh, so that rising ever anew from all downfalls, we may deserve to attain to the incorruptible Resurrection of our glorified flesh in Christ Jesus our Lord, Who lives and reigns with the Father and the Holy Ghost for ever and ever. Amen.

Three ways in which we love God

BERNARD OF CLAIRVAUX, *THE SONG OF SONGS*

❧It has been said that Christ's love is tender, wise and strong. 'I say that it is tender, since he has taken on himself our human nature; wise because he has kept himself free from all sin; and strong because he came to the point of enduring death.'

From the way in which Christ lived you can learn, Christian friend, how you should love Christ. Learn to love him tenderly, to love him wisely and to love him with strong powerful love. If you love Christ tenderly you will not be enticed away from him; if you love Christ wisely you will not be deceived and so drawn away from him; if you love Christ powerfully nothing will be able to separate you from him. Take delight in Christ for he is wisdom above everything else. Then human glory and sinful human passions will not take you away from him. Let Christ, who is the truth, so enlighten you that you are not drawn away from him by any false spirit.

Let Christ, who is the power of God, strengthen you so that you are not overcome by any enemies. Let Christian love strengthen your desire to do good; let Christ's wisdom rule you and direct your life and let steadfastness make you persevere in this. Your Christian love must not be lukewarm, timid or indiscreet. This is what is laid down in the Law, when God says, 'Love the Lord your God with all your heart and with all your soul and with all your strength' (Deuteronomy 6:5).

It seems to me that the best way to make this distinctions between the different ways to love God is as follows: the love of the heart concerns your feelings, the love of the soul centres on the decisions of your mind and the love of your strength focuses on the steadfastness of your mind. So you must love the Lord your God wholeheartedly, single-mindedly and sacrificially. As it is written in the Song of Songs, 8:6, 'love is as strong as death, its jealousy unyielding as the grave'.

...Devotion to the humanity of Christ is a great gift from the Holy Spirit. And yet I have to label this love as sinful human desire when it is compared with other more spiritual desires. For it is possible to seek after Christian graces, such as wisdom, righteousness, holiness and goodness, in the power of mere human effort. The way to remedy this is to recall these words of Paul, 'It is because of him that you are in Christ Jesus, who has become for us wisdom from God – that is, our righteousness, holiness and redemption' (1 Corinthians 1:30).

...When we love God's Son so strongly, through the help of the powerful Holy Spirit, that we do not stop seeking God's righteousness in the middle of troubles, sufferings or the threat of death, then we are loving God with all our strength. This love is spiritual love. Spiritual love is a particularly apt name to give this kind of love because its characteristic is the fullness of the Spirit. I think that this is all I need to say about the bride's words, 'No wonder the maidens love you!' (Song of Songs 1:3).

To those who scorn trembling
and quaking

GEORGE FOX, *THE JOURNAL OF GEORGE FOX*

৵ᗠAmong other services for the Lord, which then lay on me in the city of London, I was moved to give a paper to those who scorned trembling and quaking, as follows:

'The Lord of the Lord to all you that scorn trembling, and quaking; who scoff at, scorn, stone, and belch forth oaths against, those who are trembling and quaking; threatening them, and beating them. Strangers you are to all the apostles and prophets; and are of the generation that stoned them, and mocked them in those ages. You are the scoffers whom they spoke against, that are come in the last times. Be ye witnesses against yourselves. To the light in all your consciences I speak, that with it you will see yourselves to be out of the life of the holy men of God.

'...The prophet Jeremiah trembled, he shook, his bones quaked, he reeled to and fro, like a drunken man, when he saw the deceits of the priests and prophets, who had turned away from the Lord.

'Isaiah said, "Hear the word of the Lord, you that tremble at his word." And, "to this man will I look, even to him that is poor, and of contrite spirit, and trembles at my word".'

'...Habakkuk, the prophet of the Lord, trembled. And Joel said, "Blow the trumpet in Zion, and let all the inhabitants of the earth tremble: the people shall tremble." And now this trembling is witnessed by the power of the Lord. This power of the Lord is come; the trumpet is sounding; the dead are arising, and the living are praising God; the world is raging, and the scoffers are scorning; and those who witness trembling and quaking in themselves by the power of the Lord, can hardly pass up and down the streets, but with stones and blows, fists and sticks, or dogs set at them; or they are pursued with mockings and reproaches.

'…Paul, a minister of God, said, when he came to the Corinthians, that he was with them in weakness, and in fear, and in much trembling, that their faith might not stand on man's wisdom, but on God's power; in that power which made him tremble…

'Take warning, all you powers of the earth, how you persecute those whom the world nickname and call Quakers, who dwell in the eternal power of God; let the hand of the Lord be turned against you, and you be all cut off. We exalt and honour God's power, that makes the devils tremble, shakes the earth, and throws down the loftiness and haughtiness of man, which makes the beasts of the field tremble, and the earth reel to and fro.'

Spiritual transfiguration

AUGUST HERMANN FRANKE, *SERMON ON MATTHEW 17:1–9*
◈A foretaste of eternal life, a transfiguration which occurs through the Holy Spirit in the heart by faith in a spiritual way, is of much more use than the transfiguration of Jesus, which Peter, James and John witnessed. Once the disciples had seen the transfiguration they carried on with their old way of life (Matthew 18, and 20). This shows us that the spiritual transfiguration of Christ is something far more glorious and greater than the external transfiguration of Christ. We are not considering the transfiguration of the Lord before the physical eyes of the disciples as something paltry but as something great and glorious, because in it God himself witnessed about his Son. If we want to concentrate on what is helpful for our spiritual health, blessedness and salvation, we must place more emphasis on the Holy Spirit transfiguring Christ spiritually in our hearts, than on what our physical eyes might have observed about Christ's physical transfiguration.

Take note of this, then, you who pride yourself greatly that you are with the Lord Christ, who speak a great deal about him in your life, who read many prayers about him and often sing, 'Jesus My Joy, My Heart's Desire', and so on, but yet have little experience of him in your heart. Take note of this – if you know Jesus as your joy, as your heart's desire, as your treasure, as your richness, as your honour, and as everything that you desire, if you love him and truly taste him, then you will enjoy a foretaste of eternal life and experience the first drop of living water which will then become a fountain springing up into eternal life in you. Then you will be filled with the Spirit and words from Matthew 17:2 will be true for you, 'his face was shining like the sun'.

A spirit of love for both God and man

JONATHAN EDWARDS, *DISTINGUISHING MARKS OF A WORK OF THE SPIRIT OF GOD*

If the spirit that is at work among a people operates as a spirit of love to God and man, it is a sure sign that it is the Spirit of God.

The apostle insists on this sign from verse 6 to the end of the chapter: 'Beloved, let us love one another; for love is of God, and every one that loveth is born of God, and knoweth God: he that loveth not, knoweth not God; for God is love…' Here it is evident that the apostle is still comparing those two sorts of people that are influenced by the opposite kinds of spirits; and he mentioned love as a mark by which we may know who has the true spirit. This is especially evident from verses 12 and 13: 'If we love one another, God dwelleth in us, and his love is perfected in us: hereby know we that we dwell in him, and he in us, because he hath given us of his Spirit.'

In these verses love is spoken of as if it were that in which the very nature of the Holy Spirit consisted; or as if *divine love* dwelling in us, and the *Spirit of God* dwelling in us, were the same thing. It is the same in the last two verses of the previous chapter, and verse 16 of this chapter. Therefore this last mark which the apostle gives of the true Spirit he seems to speak of as the most eminent; and so insists much more largely upon it than upon all the rest; and speaks expressly of both love to God and love to men – of *love to men* in verses 7, 11, and 12; and of *love to God* in verses 17, 18, and 19; and of both together in the last two verses; and of love to men as arising from love to God, in these last two verses.

Therefore, when the spirit that is at work amongst the people tends this way, and brings many of them to high and exalting thoughts of the Divine Being, and his glorious perfections; and works in them an admiring, delightful sense of the excellence of Jesus Christ; representing him as the chief among ten thousand, and altogether lovely; and makes him precious to the soul, winning and drawing the heart with those motives and incitements to love, of which the apostle speaks in that passage of Scripture we are upon, namely the wonderful, free love of God in giving his only-begotten Son to die for us, and the wonderful love of Christ to us, who had no love to him, but were his enemies – this must be the Spirit of God. 'In this was manifested the love of God towards us, because God sent his only-begotten Son into the world, that we might live through him. Herein is love; not that we loved God, but that he loved us, and sent his Son to be the propitiation for our sins' (verses 9–10). 'And we have known, and believed, the love that God hath to us' (verse 16). 'We love him because he first loved us' (verse 19).

The spirit that excites people to love on these motives, and makes the attributes of God as revealed in the gospel, and manifested in Christ, delightful objects of contemplation; and makes the soul long after God and Christ – after their presence and communion, acquaintance with them, and conformity to them – and to live so as to please and honour them – the spirit that quells contentions among men, and gives a spirit of peace and good will, excites to acts of outward kindness, and earnest desires of the salvation of souls – and causes a delight in those that appear as the children of God, and followers of Christ; I say, when a spirit operates in this way among a people, there is the highest kind of evidence of the influence of a true and divine spirit.

Counterfeit love

Indeed there is a counterfeit love, that often appears among those who are led by a spirit of delusion. There is commonly in the wildest enthusiasts a kind of union and affection arising from self-love, occasioned by their agreeing in those things in which they greatly differ from all others, and from which they are objects of the ridicule of all the rest of mankind. This naturally will cause them so much the more to prize those peculiarities that make them the objects of others' contempt. Thus the ancient Gnostics, and the wild fanatics that appeared at the beginning of the reformation, boasted of their great love to one another; one sect of them, in particular, calling themselves the *family of love*. But this is quite another thing than that Christian love I have just described: it is only the working of a natural self-love, and no true benevolence, any more than the union and friendship which may be among a company of pirates that are at war with all the rest of the world. There is enough said in this passage about the nature of a truly Christian love, thoroughly to distinguish it from all such counterfeits. It is love that arises from apprehension of the wonderful riches of the free grace and sovereignty of God's love to us, in Christ Jesus; being attended with a sense of our own utter unworthiness, as in ourselves the enemies and haters of God and Christ, and with a renunciation of all our own excellence and righteousness. See verses 9–11 and 19.

The Christian virtue of humility
The surest character of true divine supernatural love – distinguishing it from counterfeits that arise from a natural self-love – is that the Christian virtue of *humility* shines in it; that which above all other renounces, abases, and annihilates what we term *self.* Christian love, or true charity, is a humble love. 'Charity vaunteth not itself, is not puffed up, doth not behave itself unseemly, seeketh not her own, is not easily provoked' (1 Corinthians. 13:4–5). When therefore we see love in people attended with a sense of their own littleness, vileness, weakness, and utter insufficiency; and so with self-diffidence, self-emptiness, self-renunciation, and poverty of spirit; these are the manifest tokens of the Spirit of God. He that thus dwells in love, dwells in God, and God in him. What the apostle speaks of as a great evidence of the true Spirit, is God's love or Christ's love: 'his love is perfected in us' (verse 12). What kind of love that is, we may see best in what appeared in Christ's example. The love that appeared in that Lamb of God was not only a love to friends, but to enemies, and a love attended with a meek and humble spirit. 'Learn of me,' he says, 'for I am meek and lowly in heart.'

Love and humility are two of the most contrary things in the world to the spirit of the devil, for the character of that evil spirit, above all things, consists in pride and malice.

Hindrances to revival

CHARLES FINNEY, *LECTURES ON REVIVALS OF RELIGION*

❦A revival is a work of God, and so is a crop of wheat; and God is as much dependent on the use of means in one case as in the other. And therefore a revival is as liable to be injured as a wheat field.

1. A revival will stop whenever the church believe it is going to cease. The church are the instruments with which God carries on this work. Nothing is more fatal to a revival than for its friends to predict that it is going to stop.

2. A revival will cease when Christians consent that it should cease.

3. A revival will cease when Christians become mechanical in their attempts to promote it.

4. A revival will cease whenever Christians get the idea that the work will go on without their aid. The church are co-workers with God in promoting a revival.

5. The work will cease when the church prefer to attend to their own concerns rather than God's business.

6. When Christians get proud of their great revival, it will cease.

7. The revival will stop when the church gets exhausted by labour.

8. Multitudes of Christians commit a great mistake here, in time of revival. They are so thoughtless, and have so little judgement, that they will break up all their habits of living, neglect to eat and sleep at the proper hours, and let the excitement run away with them, so that they overdo their bodies, and are so imprudent that they soon become exhausted, and it is impossible for them to continue in the work. Revivals often cease, and declensions follow, from negligence and imprudence, in this respect, on the part of those engaged in carrying them on.

A revival will cease when the church begin to speculate about abstract doctrines, which have nothing to do with practice.

9. When Christians begin to proselytizse from other Christian denominations.

10. When Christians refuse to render to the Lord according to the benefits received. God gives people up if they show a niggardly spirit.

11. When the church, in any way, grieve the Holy Spirit.

    a   When they do not feel their dependence on the Spirit.

    b   The Spirit may be grieved by a spirit of boasting of the revival.

    c   The Spirit may be grieved by saying or publishing things that are calculated to undervalue the work of God.

12. A revival may be expected to cease when Christians lose the Spirit of brotherly love.

13. A revival will decline and cease, unless Christians are frequently reconverted.

By this I mean, that Christians, in order to keep in the spirit of a revival, commonly need to be frequently convicted, and humbled, and broken down before God, and reconverted. This is something which many do not understand. But the fact is, that in a revival the Christian's heart is liable to get crusted over, and lose its exquisite relish for divine things; his unction and prevalence in prayer abates, and then he must be converted over again. It is impossible to keep him in such a state as not to do injury to the work, unless he pass through such a process every few days.

I have never laboured in revivals in company with any one who would keep in the work and be fit to manage a revival continually, who did not pass through this process of breaking down as often as once in two or three weeks. Revivals decline, commonly, because it is found impossible to make the church feel their guilt and dependence, so as to break down before God. It is important that ministers should understand this, and learn how to break down the church, and break down themselves when they need it, or else Christians will soon become mechanical in their work, and lose their fervour and their power of prevailing with God.

This is the process through which Peter passed, when he had denied the Saviour, and by which breaking down the Lord prepared him for the great work on the day of Pentecost. I was surprised a few years ago to find that the phrase 'breaking down' was a stumbling-block to certain ministers and professors of religion. They laid themselves open to the rebuke administered to Nicodemus, 'Art thou a master in Israel, and knowest not these things?' I am confident that until some of them know what it is to be 'broken down,' they never will do much more for the cause of revivals.

14. A revival cannot continue when Christians will not practise self-denial.

15. A revival will be stopped by controversies about new measures.

16. Revivals can be put down by the continued opposition of the old school, combined with a bad spirit in the new school.

17. Any diversion of the public mind will hinder a revival. Any thing that succeeds in diverting public attention, will put a stop to revival.

18. Resistance to the temperance reformation will put a stop to revivals in a church.

19. Revivals are hindered when ministers and churches take wrong ground in regard to any question involving human rights, such as the subject of slavery.

20. Another thing that hinders revivals is neglecting the claims of missions.

21. When a church rejects the calls of God upon them for educating young men for the ministry, they will hinder and destroy a revival. Look at the Presbyterian church, look at the 200,000 souls converted within ten years, and means enough to fill the world with ministers, and yet the ministry is not increasing so fast as the population of our own country.

22. Slandering revivals will often put them down.

The great revival in the days of President Edwards suffered greatly by the conduct of the church in this respect. It is to be expected that the enemies of God will revile, misrepresent, and slander revivals. But when the church herself engages in this work, and many of her most influential members are aiding and abetting in calumniating and misrepresenting a glorious work of God, it is reasonable that the Spirit should be grieved away. It cannot be denied, that this has been done to a grievous and God-dishonouring extent.

It has been estimated that in one year, since this revival commenced, 100,000 souls were converted to God in the United States. This is undoubtedly the greatest number that were ever converted in one year, since the world began. It could not be expected that, in an excitement of this extent among human beings, there should be nothing to deplore. To expect perfection in such a work as this, of such extent, and carried on by human instrumentality, is utterly unreasonable and absurd. Evils doubtless did exist, and have existed. They were to be expected of course, and guarded against as far as possible. And I do not believe the world's history can furnish one instance, in which a revival, approaching to this in extent and influence, has been attended with so few evils, and so little that is honestly to be deplored.

But how has this blessed work of God been treated? At the General Assembly, that grave body of men who represent the Presbyterian Church, in the middle of this great revival, instead of appointing a day of thanksgiving, instead of praising God for the greatness of his work, we hear from them the voice of rebuke. They sent a 'Pastoral Letter' finding fault and carping about evils. When I read what was done at that General Assembly, when I read their speeches, when I saw the pastoral letter, my soul was sick, an unutterable feeling of distress came over my mind, and I felt that God would 'visit' the Presbyterian church for conduct like this; and ever since, the glory has been departing, and departing, and revivals have been becoming less and less frequent – less and less powerful.

23. Ecclesiastical difficulties are calculated to grieve away the Spirit, and destroy revivals. President Edwards was forced to attend ecclesiastical councils, taking up his time.

24. Another thing by which revivals may be hindered, is censoriousness on either side, and especially in those who have been engaged in carrying forward a revival. The greatest hindrance to an universal Revival of the work of God, is the divided state of the church of Christ.

Look to the Cross this day!

CHARLES KINGSLEY, *GOOD FRIDAY SERMON*, 1848

෨෧Oh! Sad hearers and suffering! Anxious and weary ones! Look to the Cross this day! There hung your King. The King of sorrowing souls, and more the King of Sorrow. Ay, pain and grief, tyranny and desertion, death and hell. He has faced them one and all, and tried their strength, and taught them His, and conquered them right royally!...

And now, blessed are the poor, if they are poor in heart as well as purse, and theirs is the Kingdom of Heaven. Blessed are the hungry, if they hunger for righteousness as well as food: for

Jesus hungered, and they shall be filled. Blessed are those who mourn, if they mourn not only for their afflictions, but for their sins, and the sins of those they see around them: for on this day, Jesus mourned for our sins: on this day He was made sin for us who knew no sin; and they shall be comforted. Blessed are those who are ashamed of themselves and humble themselves before God this day; for on this day Jesus humbled Himself for us, and they shall be exalted. Blessed are the forsaken and despised. Did not all men forsake Jesus this day, in His hour of need?…

Rejoice and trust on, for after sorrow shall come joy. Trust on; for in man's weakness God's strength shall be made perfect. Trust on, for death is the gate of life. Endure on to the end, and possess your souls in patience for a little while, and that perhaps a very little while. Death comes swiftly, and more swiftly still, perhaps, the day of the Lord. The deeper the sorrow, the nearer the salvation.

The night is darkest before the dawn;
When the pain is sorest, the child is born,
And the day of the Lord at hand!

'By grace are ye saved through faith; and that not of yourselves: it is the gift of God.'

C.H. SPURGEON, SERMON PREACHED AT THE METROPOLITAN TABERNACLE, NEWINGTON, LONDON.

⟋Salvation may be called Theodora, or God's gift: and each saved soul may be surnamed Dorothea, which is another form of the same expression. Multiply your phrases, and expand your expositions; but salvation truly traced to its well-head is all contained in the gift unspeakable, the free, unmeasured benison of love.

Salvation is the gift of God, in opposition to a wage. When a man pays another his wage, he does what is right; and no one dreams of praising him for it. But we praise God for salvation because it is not the payment of debt, but the gift of grace. No man enters eternal life on earth, or in heaven, as his due: it is the gift of God. We say, 'nothing is freer than a gift'. Salvation is so purely, so absolutely a gift of God, that nothing can be more free. God gives it because he chooses to give it, according to that grand text which has made many a man bite his lip in wrath, 'I will have mercy on whom I will have mercy, I will have compassion on whom I will have compassion.' You are all guilty and condemned, and the great King pardons whom he wills from among you. This is his royal prerogative. He saves in infinite sovereignty of grace…

Salvation is the gift of God: that is, it is eternally secure in opposition to the gifts of men, which soon pass away. 'Not as the world giveth, give I unto you,' says our Lord Jesus. If my Lord Jesus gives you salvation at this moment, you have it, and you have it forever. He will never take it back again; and if he does not take it from you, who can? If he saves you now through faith, you are saved; so saved that you shall never perish, neither shall any pluck you out of his hand. May it be so with every one of us! Amen.

'Holiness, without which no man shall see the Lord,' (Hebrews 12:14)

J.C. RYLE, *HOLINESS*

ᥫThis text opens up a subject of deep importance. That subject is practical holiness. It suggests a question which demands the attention of all professing Christians – Are we holy? Shall we see the Lord?

That question concerns all ranks and conditions of men. Some are rich and some are poor – some learned and some unlearned – some masters, and some servants; but there is no rank or condition in life in which a man ought not to be holy. Are we?

I ask to be heard today about this question. How stands the account between our souls and God? In this hurrying, bustling world, let us stand still for a few minutes and consider the matter of holiness. I believe I might have chosen a subject more popular and pleasant. I am sure I might have found one more easy to handle. But I feel deeply I could not have chosen one more profitable to our souls. It is a solemn thing to hear the Word of God saying, 'Without holiness no man shall see the Lord' (Hebrews. 12:14).

I shall endeavour, by God's help, to examine what true holiness is, and the reason why it is so needful. In conclusion, I shall try to point out the only way in which holiness can be attained.

1. First, then, let me try to show what true practical holiness is – what sort of persons are those whom God calls holy.

A man may go great lengths, and yet never reach true holiness. It is not knowledge – Balaam had that: nor great profession – Judas Iscariot had that: nor doing many things – Herod had that: nor zeal for certain matters in religion – Jehu had that: nor morality and outward respectability of conduct – the young ruler had that: nor taking pleasure in hearing preachers – the Jews in Ezekiel's time had that: nor keeping company with godly people – Joab and Gehazi and Demas had that. Yet none of these was holy! These things alone are not holiness. A man may have any one of them, and yet never see the Lord.

What then is true practical holiness?…

a) Holiness is the habit of being of one mind with God, according as we find His mind described in Scripture. It is the habit of agreeing in God's judgement – hating what He hates – loving what He loves – and measuring everything in this world by the standard of His Word. He who most entirely agrees with God, he is the most holy man.

b) A holy man will endeavour to shun every known sin, and to keep every known commandment. He will feel what David felt when he said, 'I esteem all Thy precepts concerning all things to be right, and I hate every false way' (Psalm 119:128).

c) A holy man will strive to be like our Lord Jesus Christ. He will not only live the life of faith in Him, and draw from Him all his daily peace and strength, but he will also labour to have the mind that was in Him, and to be 'conformed to His image' (Romans. 8:29).

d) A holy man will follow after meekness, long-suffering, gentleness, patience, kind tempers, government of his tongue. He will bear much, forbear much, overlook much, and be slow to talk of standing on his rights. We see a bright example of this in the behaviour of David when Shimei cursed him – and of Moses when Aaron and Miriam spake against him (2 Samuel. 16:10; Numbers. 12:3).

e) A holy man will follow after temperance and self-denial. He will labour to mortify the desires of his body – to crucify his flesh with his affections and lusts – to curb his passions – to restrain his carnal inclinations, lest at any time they break loose.

f) A holy man will follow after charity and brotherly kindness. He will endeavour to observe the golden rule of doing as he would have men do to him, and speaking as he would have men speak to him. He will be full of affection towards his brethren – towards their bodies, their property, their characters, their feelings, their souls. 'He that loveth another,' says Paul, 'hath fulfilled the law' (Romans. 13:8).

g) A holy man will follow after a spirit of mercy and benevolence towards others. He will not stand all the day idle. He will not be content with doing no harm – he will try to do good.

h) A holy man will follow after purity of heart. He will dread all filthiness and uncleanness of spirit, and seek to avoid all things that might draw him into it.

i) A holy man will follow after the fear of God.

j) A holy man will follow after humility. He will desire, in lowliness of mind, to esteem all others better than himself. He will see more evil in his own heart than in any other in the world. Holy Bradford, that faithful martyr of Christ, would sometimes finish his letters with these words, 'A most miserable sinner, John Bradford.' Good old Mr. Grimshaw's last words, when he lay on his death-bed, were these, 'Here goes an unprofitable servant.'

k) A holy man will follow after faithfulness in all the duties and relations in life. He will try, not merely to fill his place as well as others who take no thought for their souls, but even better, because he has higher motives, and more help than they. Those words of Paul should never be forgotten, 'Whatever ye do, do it heartily, as unto the Lord,' – 'Not slothful in business, fervent in spirit, serving the Lord' (Colossians. 3:23; Romans. 12:11).

l) Last, but not least, a holy man will follow after spiritual mindedness. He will endeavour to set his affections entirely on things above, and to hold things on earth with a very loose hand. He will value every thing and place and company, just in proportion as it draws him nearer to God. He will enter into something of David's feeling, when he says, 'My soul followeth hard after Thee.' 'Thou art my portion' (Psalms 63:8; 119:57).

Such is the outline of holiness which I venture to sketch out. Such is the character which those who are called 'holy' follow after. Such are the main features of a holy man.

MARTYRS AND MARTYRDOMS

❦

Ignatius of Antioch

BEFORE HIS MARTYRDOM

☙Father, make us more like Jesus. Help us to bear difficulty, pain, disappointment and sorrow, knowing that in your perfect working and design you can use such bitter experiences to mould our characters and make us more like our Lord. We look with hope to the day when we will be completely like Christ, because we will see him as he is…

I am God's wheat. May I be grounded by the teeth of the wild beasts until I become the fine wheat bread that is Christ's. My passions are crucified, there is no heat in my flesh, a stream flows murmuring inside me; deep down in me it says: Come to the Father.

Polycarp

MARTYRIUM POLICARPI

Then, when he had been brought in, the proconsul asked him if he was Polycarp. And when he confessed, he would have persuaded him to deny, saying, Have respect unto thine age, and other things like these, as is their custom to say: Swear by the fortunes of Caesar; Repent; Say, Away with the Atheists. [People who refused to sacrifice to the gods were termed 'atheists'.] But Polycarp, when he had looked with a grave face at all the multitude of lawless heathen in the arena, having beckoned unto them with his hand, sighed, and looking up unto heaven, said, Away with the Atheists!

And when the proconsul pressed him, and said, Swear, and I will release thee, revile Christ; Polycarp said, Eighty and six years have I served him, and in nothing hath he wronged me; and how, then, can I blaspheme my King, who saved me?

...The proconsul said unto him, I have wild beasts; I will deliver thee unto them, unless thou repentest. But he said, Call them, for repentance from the better to the worse is impossible for us; but it is a good thing to change from evil deeds to just ones.

But he said again unto him, I will cause thee to be consumed by fire if thou despisest the wild beasts, unless thou repentest. But Polycarp said, Thou threatenest me with fire that burneth but for a season, and is soon quenched. For thou art ignorant of the fire of the judgement to come, and of the eternal punishment reserved for the wicked. But why delayest thou? Bring whatever thou wishest.

The multitude quickly collecting logs and brushwood from the workshops and baths, the Jews especially lending their services zealously for this purpose, as is their custom.

But when the pyre was ready, having put off all his garments, and having loosed his girdle, he essayed to take off his shoes; not being in the habit of doing this previously, because each of the faithful used to strive which should be the first to touch his body, for, on account of his good conversation, he was, even before his martyrdom, adorned with every good gift.

Straightway, therefore, there were put around him the implements prepared for the pyre. And when they were about besides to nail him to it, he said, Suffer me thus, for he who gave me to abide the fire will also allow me, without the security of your nails, to remain on the pyre without moving.

They, therefore, did not nail him, but bound him. But he, having placed his hands behind him, and being bound, like a notable ram appointed for offering out of a great flock, prepared as a whole burnt-offering acceptable unto God, having looked up unto heaven, said, O Lord God Almighty, Father of thy beloved and blessed Son Jesus Christ, through whom we have received our knowledge concerning thee, the God of angels and powers, and of the whole creation, and of all the race of the just who lived before thee, I thank thee that thou hast deemed me worthy of this day and hour, that I should have my portion in the number of the martyrs, in the cup of thy Christ, unto the resurrection of eternal life, both of the soul and body, in the incorruptibility of the Holy Spirit. Among these may I be received before thee this day as a rich and acceptable sacrifice, even as thou hast prepared and made manifest beforehand, and hast fulfilled, thou who art the unerring and true God.

On this account, and concerning all things, I praise thee, I bless thee, I glorify thee, together with the eternal and heavenly Jesus Christ thy beloved Son, with whom to thee and the Holy Spirit be glory both now and for ever. Amen.

And when he had uttered the Amen, and had finished his prayer, the men who superintended the fire kindled it.

...We pray, brethren, that you may fare well, walking by the word of the gospel of Jesus Christ, with whom be glory to God and the Father, and the Holy Spirit, for the salvation of the holy elect, even as the blessed Polycarp hath born witness, in whose steps may we be found in the kingdom of Jesus Christ.

A threefold crown

JOHN CHRYSOSTOM, *EULOGY FOR THE MARTYR IGNATIUS*

⚬Sumptuous and splendid entertainers give frequent and constant entertainments, alike to display their own wealth, and to show goodwill to their acquaintance. So also the grace of the Spirit, affording us a proof of his own power, and displaying much goodwill towards the friends of God, sets before us successively and constantly the tables of the martyrs...

Ignatius presided over the Church among us nobly, and with such carefulness as Christ desires. For that which Christ declared to be the highest standard and rule of the Episcopal office, did this man display by his deeds. For having heard Christ saying, the good shepherd layeth down his life for the sheep, with all courage he did lay it down for the sheep.

He held true converse with the apostles and drank of spiritual fountains. What kind of person then is it likely that he was who had been reared, and who had everywhere held converse with them, and had shared with them truths both lawful and unlawful to utter, and who seemed to them worthy of so great a dignity? The time again came on, which demanded courage; and a soul which despised all things present, glowed with Divine love, and valued things unseen before the things which are seen; and he lay aside the flesh with as much ease as one would put off a garment. What then shall we speak of first? The teaching of the apostles which he gave proof of throughout, or his indifference to this present life, or the strictness of his virtue, with which he administered his rule over the Church; which shall we first call to mind? The martyr or the bishop or the apostle. For the grace of the spirit having woven a threefold crown, thus bound it on his holy head, yea rather a manifold crown. For if any one will consider them carefully, he will find each of the crowns, blossoming with other crowns for us...

For now, by the grace of God, there is no danger for bishops, but deep peace on all sides, and we all enjoy a calm, since the Word of piety has been extended to the ends of the world, and our rulers keep the faith with strictness. But then there was nothing of this, but wherever any one might look, precipices and pitfalls, and wars, and fightings, and dangers; both rulers, and kings, and people and cities and nations, and men at home and abroad, laid snares for the faithful. And this was not the only serious thing, but also the fact that many of the believers themselves, inasmuch as they tasted for the first time strange doctrines, stood in need of great indulgence, and were still in a somewhat feeble condition and were often upset. And this was a thing which used to grieve the teachers, no less than the fightings without, nay rather much more. For the fightings without, and the plottings, afforded much pleasure to them on account of the hope of the rewards awaiting them. On this account the apostles returned from the presence of the Sanhedrin rejoicing because they had been beaten; and Paul cries out, saying: 'I rejoice in my sufferings,' and he glories in his afflictions everywhere. But the wounds of those at home, and the fails of the brethren, do not suffer them to breathe again, but always, like some most heavy yoke, continually oppress and afflict the neck of their soul. Hear at least how Paul, thus rejoicing in sufferings, is bitterly pained about these. 'For who, saith he, is weak, and I am not weak? who is offended, and I burn not?' and again, 'I fear lest when I come I shall find you not such as I would, and I be found of you such as ye would not,' and a little afterwards, 'Lest when I come again to you, God humble me, and I shall mourn many of those who have sinned before, and have not repented, of their uncleanness, and wantonness, and fornication which they have committed.' And throughout thou seest that he is in tears and lamentations on account of members of the household, and evermore fearing and trembling for the believers... For if the oversight of the Church now furnishes much weariness and work to those who govern it, consider how double and treble and manifold was the work then, when there were dangers and fighting and snares, and fear continually. It is not possible to set forth in words the difficulty which those saints then encountered, but he alone will know it who comes to it by experience.

Not only today, therefore, but every day let us go forth to him, plucking spiritual fruits from him. For it is, it is possible for him who comes hither with faith to gather the fruit of many good things... Wherefore I beseech you all, if any is in despondency, if in disease, if under insult, if in any other circumstance of this life, if in the depth of sins, let him come hither with faith, and he will lay aside all those things, and will return with much joy, having procured a lighter conscience from the sight alone. But more, it is not only necessary that those who are in affliction should come hither, but if any one be in cheerfulness, in glory, in power, in much assurance towards God, let not this man despise the benefit. For coming hither and beholding this saint, he will keep these noble possessions unmoved, persuading his own soul to be moderate by the recollection of this man's mighty deeds, and not suffering his conscience by the mighty deeds to be lifted up to any self conceit. And it is no slight thing for those in prosperity not to be puffed up at their good fortune, but to know how to bear their prosperity with moderation, so that the trea-sure is serviceable to all, the resting place is suitable, for the fallen, in order that they may escape from their temptations, for the fortunate, that their success may remain secure, for those in weakness indeed, that they may return to health, and for the healthy, that they may not fall into weakness. Considering all which things, let us prefer this way of spending our time, to all delight, all pleasure, in order that rejoicing at once, and profiling, we may be able to become partakers with these saints, both of their dwelling and of their home, ... through the grace and lov-ing kindness of our Lord Jesus Christ, with whom be glory to the Father with the Holy Spirit, now and always forever and ever, amen.

In fearing not to fear, and in not fearing to fear

AUGUSTINE, *SERMON PREACHED ON A FESTIVAL OF MARTYRS*

'Be not afraid of them that kill the body' (Matthew 10:28)
ഌThe Divine oracles which have just been read teach us in fearing not to fear, and in not fearing to fear. Ye observed when the Holy Gospel was being read, that our Lord God before He died for us, would have us to be firm; and this by admonishing us 'not' to fear, and withal to fear. For he said, 'Fear not them which kill the body, but are not able to kill the soul.' See where He advised us not to fear. See now where He advised us to fear. 'But,' said he, 'fear Him who hath power to destroy both body and soul in hell.' Let us fear therefore, that we may not fear. Fear seems to be linked to cowardice. It seems to be the character of the weak, not the strong. But see what said the Scripture, 'The fear of the

Lord is the hope of strength.' Let us then fear, that we may not fear; that is, let us fear prudently, that we may not fear vainly. The holy martyrs on the occasion of whose solemnity this lesson was read out of the Gospel, in fearing, feared not; because in fearing God, they did not regard men.

For what need a man fear from man? And what is that whereby one man should cause another fear, since both of them are men? ... For he is but a man, and he threatens another man, a creature, another creature; only the one puffed up under his Creator's eye, and the other fleeing for refuge to the same Creator.

Let the stout Martyr then, as he stands a man before another man, say, 'I do not fear, because I fear.' Thou canst not do what thou art threatening, unless He will; but what He threateneth, none can hinder Him from doing ... Behold (I am using the words of a Martyr), behold, I say, not even on account of my body do I fear thy threats. My body indeed is subject to thy power; but even the hairs of my head are numbered by my Creator. Why should I fear lest I lose my body, who cannot even lose a hair? How shall he not have a care of my body, to whom my meanest things are so well known? This body which may be wounded and slain will for a time be ashes, but it will be for ever immortal. But to whom shall this be? To whom shall the body be restored for life eternal, even though it have been slain, destroyed, and scattered to the winds? to whom shall it be so restored? To him who has not been afraid to lay down his own life, since he does not fear, lest his body should be slain...

The body is dead without the soul, and that the soul is dead without God. Every man without God hath a dead soul. Thou dost bewail the dead: bewail the sinner rather, bewail rather the ungodly man, bewail the unbeliever. It is written, 'The mourning for the dead is seven days; for a fool and an ungodly man all the days of his life.' What, is there nothing of Christian compassion in thee; that thou mournest for a body from which the soul is gone, and mournest not for the soul, from which God is departed? Let the Martyr remembering this make answer to him that threatens him, 'Why dost thou force me to deny Christ?' Wouldest thou then force me to deny the truth? And if I will not, what wilt thou do? Thou wilt assault my body, that my soul shall depart from it; but this same soul of mine has its body only for the soul's sake. It is not so foolish or unwise. Thou wouldest wound my body; but wouldest thou, that through fear lest thou shouldest wound my body, and my soul should depart from it, I should wound mine own soul, and my God should depart from it? Fear not then, O Martyr, the sword of thy executioner; fear only thine own tongue, lest thou do execution upon thine own self, and slay, not thy body, but thy soul. Fear for thy soul, lest it die in hell-fire.

Therefore said the Lord, 'Who hath power to slay both body and soul in hell-fire.' How? when the ungodly shall be cast into hell-fire, will his body and his soul burn there? Everlasting pun-ishment will be the death of the body; the absence of God will be the death of the soul. Wouldest thou know what the death of the soul is? Understand the Prophet who said, 'Let the ungodly be taken away, that he may not see the glory of the Lord.' Let the soul then fear its proper death, and not fear the death of its body. Because if it fear its own death, and so live in its God, by not offending and thrusting Him away from him, it will be found worthy so to receive its body again at the end; not unto everlast-ing punishment, as the ungodly, but unto life eternal, as the right-eous. By fearing this death, and loving that life, did the Martyrs, in hope of the promises of God, and in contempt of the threats of persecutors, attain themselves to be crowned with God, and have left to us the celebration of these solemnities.

You are now going to burn a goose

JOHN FOXE, *THE BOOK OF MARTYRS,* REVISED WITH NOTES
AND AN APPENDIX BY W. BRAMLEY-MOORE

Huss received the sentence without the slightest emotion; and then knelt down, lifted up his eyes towards heaven, exclaiming, with the magnanimity of a primitive martyr, 'May thy infinite mercy, O my God! pardon this injustice of mine enemies. Thou knowest the injustice of my accusations: how deformed with crimes I have been represented; how I have been oppressed with worthless witnesses, and a false condemnation; yet, O my God! let that mercy of thine, which no tongue can express, prevail with thee not to avenge my wrongs.'

But these excellent sentences were received as so many expressions of treason, and only tended to inflame his adversaries. Accordingly, the bishops appointed by the council stripped him of his priestly garments, degraded him, and put a paper mitre on his head, on which they painted three devils, with this inscription: 'Heresiarch' [Heretic]. This mockery was received by the martyr with an air of unconcern, and seemed to give him dignity rather than disgrace. A serenity appeared in his looks, which indicated that his soul was approaching the realms of everlasting happiness; and when the bishop urged him to recant, he turned to the people and addressed them thus.

'These lords and bishops do counsel me that I should confess before you all that I have erred; which thing, if it might be done with the infamy and reproach of many only, they might, peradventure, easily persuade me to do; but now I am in the sight of the Lord my God, without whose great displeasure I could not do that which they require. For I well know that I never taught any of those things which they have falsely accused me of, but I have always preached, taught, written, and thought contrary thereunto. Should I by this my example trouble so many consciences, endued with the most certain knowledge of the Scriptures and of the gospel of our Lord Jesus Christ? I will never do it, neither commit any such offence, that I should seem to esteem this vile carcass appointed unto death more than their health and salvation.'

At this most godly word he was forced again to hear that he did obstinately persevere in his pernicious errors.

After the ceremony of degradation the bishops delivered him to the emperor, who handed him over to the Duke of Bavaria. His books were burnt at the gates of the church; and on July 6th he was led to the suburbs of Constance to be burnt alive.

Having reached the place of execution, he fell on his knees, sung several portions from the Psalms, and looked steadfastly towards heaven, saying, 'Into thy hands, O Lord! do I commit my spirit: thou hast redeemed me, O most good and faithful God.'

As soon as the chain was put around him at the stake, he said, with a smiling countenance, 'My Lord Jesus Christ was bound with a harder chain than this for my sake: why, then, should I be ashamed of this old rusty one?' Then he prayed: 'Lord Jesus Christ, it is for the sake of the gospel and the preaching of the word that I patiently undergo this ignominious death.'

When the faggots were piled around him, the Duke of Bavaria was officious as to desire him to abjure. 'No,' he said, 'I never preached any doctrine of an evil tendency; and what I taught with my lips I now seal with my blood.' He then said to the executioner, 'You are now going to burn a goose (the meaning of Huss's name in Bohemian), but in a century you will have a swan whom you can neither roast nor boil.' If this were spoken in prophecy, he must have alluded to Martin Luther, who came about a hundred years after him, and had a swan for his arms.

As soon as the faggots were lighted, the martyr sang a hymn, with so cheerful a voice, that he was heard above the cracklings of the fire and the noise of the multitude. At length his voice was interrupted by the flames, which soon put an end to his existence. His ashes were collected, and, by order of the council, thrown into the Rhine, lest his adherents should honour them as relics.

Thomas Cranmer

JOHN FOXE, *THE BOOK OF MARTYRS,* REVISED WITH NOTES AND AN APPENDIX BY W. BRAMLEY-MOORE
[Cranmer was Archbishop of Canterbury and compiler of the Book of Common Prayer. In Queen Mary's reign he was tried and condemned to be executed as a heretic. Before his execution, he signed recantations of the beliefs which he continued to hold which were really his. Hence the significance of his later statement: 'I recant of my recantations.']

⊷Thomas Cranmer was born at Aslacton, in Nottinghamshire, on the 2nd July, 1489. His family, who traced their descent from the time of the Norman Conquest, had resided in that town for many generations. On his father's death, in 1503, his mother placed him at Jesus College, in Cambridge, where he applied himself with great diligence to his studies, particularly to those of Greek, Hebrew, and theology. In 1510 he was chosen a fellow of his college, but in consequence of his marriage taking place shortly afterwards, he lost his fellowship. On this he became a reader in Buckingham College [now known as Magdalene College].

While Cranmer was at Cambridge, the vexed question of King Henry VIII's divorce with Lady Catherine of Aragon arose.

The cardinals Campeggio and Wolsey had been appointed as Papal commissioners to decide the knotty point, but finding themselves beset with difficulties, from Henry's urgency on the one hand, and from the fact that Catherine was aunt to the Emperor Charles V, on the other, procrastinated matters, in the usual hope that time and the chapter of accidents would befriend them, and bring the desired solution. The king, however, became enraged at the delay. He accordingly dismissed Cardinal Campeggio, and visited Waltham Abbey, in Essex, where Cranmer was staying, because of the plague. At Waltham, Dr Gardiner, later Bishop of Winchester, and Fox, subsequently Bishop of Hereford, who were in attendance on the king, met Cranmer, and the conversation turned upon the pending controversy of the time.

In the course of conversation Cranmer suggested the expediency of 'trying the question by the Word of God'; and that the matter might be as well settled in England by the universities as in Rome, or in any foreign court. When Fox, who was Royal almoner, repeated the substance of the conversation to the king, the king swore 'that man had the right sow by the ear'. Cranmer was accordingly summoned to court, received into favour, and, on the disgrace of Wolsey, promoted to the see of Canterbury.

It is not for us to enter into a minute analysis of the difficulties of the archbishop's position, or of the motives which influenced his conduct at certain critical junctures. Candour obliges us to admit that there are many passages in his life which a faithful biographer would desire to treat with charity. At the same time, allowance must be made for the dilemmas of a giant mind struggling to free itself from the shackles of association, education, and prejudice, and for its gradual advance towards the goal of truth. Cranmer's opinions passed through various transition states; and his mind was extricated from erroneous doctrines on the sacramental presence only by slow degrees. His conduct, with reference to his oath of consecration, the divorce of Anne Boleyn, the condemnation of John Frith and Joan of Kent, is open to the apologies of the casuist or the censure of the rigid moralist; but, considering that he was educated in the Church of Rome, we may well wonder at his grasp of truth and his advance towards the light. To him, as much as to any other, is England indebted for the legacy of an open Bible, and his master mind advanced the reformation of the Church of England to almost her present position, and moulded her with a wisdom full of homage to truth, yet with a deference to antiquity, when adjudged blameless.

We now pass over those events of his public career and come to the close of his eventful life. In September, 1555, Dr Brooks, Bishop of Gloucester, came with authority from Cardinal Pole to judge Cranmer. Brooks required Cranmer to appear before the Pope within eighty days. In February, 1556, Bonner and Thirleby were sent to degrade him for his contumacy in not going to Rome, although he was all the while kept in prison. Cranmer denied that the Pope had any authority over him, and appealed from his sentence to a free general council.

But now many devices were set on foot to make him recant: both English and Spanish divines had many conferences with him, and great hopes were given him, not only of life, but of preferment, if he would do it; and these, at last, had a fatal effect upon him, for he signed a recantation of all his former opinions, and concluded it with a protestation that he had done it freely, for the discharge of his conscience. The queen, however, was resolved to sacrifice him to her resentments; and, she said, it was good for his own soul that he repented; but since he had been the chief spreader of heresy over the nation, it was necessary to make him a public example. Accordingly the writ was sent down to burn him, and, after some stop had been made in the execution of it, new orders came for doing it suddenly. This was kept from

Cranmer's knowledge, for they intended to carry him to the stake without giving him any notice, and so hoped to make him die in despair; yet he, suspecting somewhat, wrote a long paper, containing a confession of his faith, such as his conscience, and not his fears, had dictated.

He was carried to St Mary's on 21st March, where Dr Cole preached, and vindicated the queen's justice in condemning Cranmer; but magnified his conversion much, and ascribed it to God's Spirit. He gave him great hopes of heaven, and promised him all the relief that masses could bring.

All this time, with great grief, Cranmer stood hearing his sermon: one while lifting up his hands and eyes unto heaven, and then again, for shame, letting them down to earth, while the tears gushed from his eyes. Great commiseration and pity moved all men's hearts, that beheld so heavy a countenance, and such abundance of tears in an old man of so reverend dignity.

After Cole had ended his sermon, he called back the people to prayers that were ready to depart. 'Brethren,' he said, 'lest any man should doubt of this man's earnest conversion and repentance, you shall hear him speak before you, and, therefore, I pray you, Mr Cranmer, to perform that now which you promised not long ago – namely, that you would openly express the true and undoubted profession of your faith, that you may take away all suspicion from men, and that all men may understand that you are a catholic indeed.'

'I will do it,' said the archbishop, 'and that with a good will,' and rising up, and putting off his cap, he began to speak thus unto the people:

Good people – my dearly beloved brethren in Christ, I beseech you most heartily to pray for me to Almighty God, that he will forgive me all my sins and offences, which are without number, and

*great above measure. But yet one thing grieveth my conscience
more than all the rest, whereof, God willing, I intend to speak
more hereafter. But how great and how many soever my sins be, I
beseech you to pray to God of his mercy to pardon and forgive
them all.'*

And here, kneeling down, he said the following prayer:

*O Father of heaven, O Son of God, Redeemer of the world, O
Holy Ghost, three persons and one God, have mercy upon me,
most wretched caitiff and miserable sinner. I have offended both
against heaven and earth more than my tongue can express.
Whither, then, may I go, or whither shall I flee? To heaven I may
be ashamed to lift up mine eyes, and in earth I find no place of
refuge or succour. To thee, therefore, O Lord, do I run; to thee do
I humble myself, saying, O Lord my God, my sins be great, but
yet have mercy upon me for thy great mercy. The great mystery
that God became man was not wrought for little or few offences.
Thou didst not give thy Son, O heavenly Father, unto death for
small sins only, but for all the greatest sins of the world, so that
the sinner return to thee with his whole heart, as I do at this
present. Wherefore have mercy on me, O God, whose property is
always to have mercy; have mercy upon me, O Lord, for they
great mercy. I crave nothing for mine own merits, but for
thy name's sake. And now, O Father of heaven, hallowed be thy
name.*

And after repeating the Lord's Prayer, he continued:

*Every man, good people, desireth at the time of his death to give
some good exhortation, that others may remember the same before
their death, and be the better thereby; so I beseech God grant me*

that I may speak something at this my departing, whereby God may be glorified, and you edified.

First, it is a heavy cause to see that so many folk so much dote upon the love of this false world, and be so careful for it, that of the love of God, or the world to come, they seem to care very little or nothing. Therefore, this shall be my first exhortation: That you set not your minds over much upon this deceitful world, but upon God, and upon the world to come, and to learn to know what this lesson meaneth which St John teacheth, that the love of this world is hatred against God.

The second exhortation is, That next unto God you obey your King and Queen, willingly and gladly.

The third exhortation is, That you love altogether like brethren and sisters.

The fourth exhortation shall be to them that have great substance and riches of this world, That they will well consider and weigh Luke 18:24, 1 John 3:17 and James 5:1–3. Let them that be rich ponder well these three sentences; for if they ever had occasion to show their charity, they have it now at this present, the poor people being so many, and victuals so dear.

And now, forasmuch as I am come to the last end of my life, whereupon hangeth all my life past and all my life to come, either to live with my master Christ for ever in joy, or else to be in pain for ever with wicked devils in hell, and I see before my eyes presently either heaven ready to receive me, or else hell ready to swallow me up; I shall therefore declare to you my very faith how I believe, without any colour of dissimulation, for now is no time to dissemble, whatsoever I have said or written in times past.

First, I believe in God the Father Almighty, maker of heaven and earth etc. And I believe every article of the catholic faith, every word and sentence taught by our Saviour Jesus Christ, his apostles and prophets, in the New and Old Testament.

And now I come to the great thing, that so much troubleth my conscience, more than any thing that ever I did or said in my whole life; and this is the setting abroad of a writing contrary to the Truth; which now here I renounce and refuse, as things written with my hand, contrary to the truth which I thought in my heart, and written for fear of death, and to save my life, if it might be; and that is, all such bills and papers which I have written or signed with my hand since my degradation, wherein I have written many things untrue. And forasmuch as my hand offended, writing contrary to my heart, my hand shall first be punished therefore; for, may I come to the fire it shall be first burned.

[In the two sentences that followed he abjured the Pope and stood by his former book on the sacrament.] There was an immediate outcry at this unexpected recantation of his recantations, and he was pulled down from the stage and hustled along the street to the ditch opposite Balliol College, where Latimer and Ridley had been burned.

[After kneeling in prayer he stripped himself of his shirt, bared his head and feet, shook hands with some of the bystanders and so went to the stake.]

And when the wood was kindled, and the fire began to burn near him, stretching out his arm, he put his right hand into the flame, which he held so steadfast and immovable that all men might see his hand burned before his body was touched. His body did so abide the burning of the flame, with such constancy and steadfastness, that standing always in one place, without moving his body, he seemed to move no more than the stake to which he was bound: his eyes were lifted up unto heaven, and often times he repented his unworthy right hand, so long as his voice would suffer him: and using often the words of Stephen, 'Lord Jesus receive my spirit'; in the greatness of the flame he gave up the ghost.

RULES AND CATECHISMS

෴

Be single-minded in your imitation
of Christ

RULE OF ST COLUMBA
[This rule, attributed to St Columba, reflects the spirit of early
Irish monasticism.]

෴Be alone in a separate place near a chief city, if thy conscience
is not prepared to be in common with the crowd.

Be always single-minded in your imitation of Christ and the
Evangelists.

Whatsoever little or much thou possessest of anything,
whether clothing, or food, or drink, let it be at the command of
the senior and at his disposal, for it is not befitting a religious to
have any distinction of property with his own free brother.

Let a fast place, with one door, enclose thee.

A few religious men to converse with thee of God and
his Testament; to visit thee on days of solemnity; to strengthen
thee in the Testaments of God, and the narratives of the
Scriptures.

A person too who would talk with thee in idle words, or of the world; or who murmurs at what he cannot remedy or prevent, but who would distress thee more should he be a tattler between friends and foes, thou shalt not admit him to thee, but at once give him thy benediction should he deserve it.

Let thy servant be a discreet, religious, not tale-telling man, who is to attend continually on thee, with moderate labour of course, but always ready.

Yield submission to every rule that is of devotion.

A mind prepared for red martyrdom [that is, death for the faith].

A mind fortified and steadfast for white martyrdom [that is, ascetic practices]. Forgiveness from the heart of every one. Constant prayers for those who trouble thee.

Fervour in singing the office for the dead, as if every faithful dead was a particular friend of thine.

Hymns for souls to be sung standing.

Let thy vigils be constant from eve to eve, under the direction of another person.

Three labours in the day, viz., prayers, work, and reading.

The work to be divided into three parts, viz., thine own work, and the work of thy place, as regards its real wants; secondly, thy share of the brethren's work; lastly, to help the neighbours, viz., by instruction or writing, or sewing garments, or whatever labour they may be in want of, as the Lord says, 'You shall not appear before me empty.'

Everything in its proper order; for no one is crowned except he who has striven lawfully.

Follow alms-giving before all things.

Take not of food till thou art hungry.

Sleep not till thou feelest desire.

Speak not except on business.

Every increase which comes to thee in lawful meals, or in

wearing apparel, give it for pity to the brethren that want it, or to the poor in like manner.

The love of God with all thy heart and all thy strength;

The love of thy neighbour as thyself.

Abide in the Testament of God throughout all times.

Thy measure of prayer shall be until thy tears come;

Or thy measure of work of labour till thy tears come;

Or thy measure of thy work of labour … until thy perspiration often comes, if thy tears are not free.

Love God

JOHN COLET, *CATECHISM FOR CHILDREN*

Love God.

Thrust down pride.

Forgive gladly.

Be sober of meat and drink.

Use honest company.

Reverence thine elders.

Trust in God's mercy.

Be always well occupied.

Lose no time.

Falling down, despair not.

Ever take a fresh, new, good purpose.

Persevere constantly.

Wash clean.

Be no sluggard.

Awake quickly.

Enrich thee with virtue.

Learn diligently.

Teach what thou hast learned, lovingly.

Act of commitment

MATTHEW HENRY, *ACT OF COMMITMENT*
[Taught to Matthew Henry by his father.]

I take God the Father to be my God;
I take God the Son to be my Saviour;
I take God the Holy Ghost to be my Sanctifier;
I take the Word of God to be my rule;
I take the people of God to be my people;
And I do hereby dedicate and yield my whole self to the Lord:
And I do this deliberately, freely, and for ever. Amen.

Good deeds

JOHN WESLEY'S RULE
Do all the good you can,
By all the means you can,
In all the ways you can,
In all the places you can,
At all the times you can,
To all the people you can,
As long as ever you can.

COMMENTARIES

❧◦◦❧

Preface to Romans

MARTIN LUTHER, PREFACE TO THE EPISTLE TO THE ROMANS
[Luther's preface and commentary on Paul's letter to the Romans originated as lectures to his theological students at Wittenberg which were delivered in 1515.]

❧This letter is truly the most important piece in the New Testament. It is purest Gospel. It is well worth a Christian's while not only to memorize it word for word but also to occupy himself with it daily, as though it were the daily bread of the soul. It is impossible to read or to meditate on this letter too much or too well. The more one deals with it, the more precious it becomes and the better it tastes. Therefore I want to carry out my service and, with this preface, provide an introduction to the letter, insofar as God gives me the ability, so that every one can gain the fullest possible understanding of it. Up to now it has been darkened by glosses and by many a useless comment, but it is in itself a bright light, almost bright enough to illumine the entire Scripture.

To begin with, we have to become familiar with the vocabulary of the letter and know what St Paul means by the words law, sin, grace, faith, justice, flesh, spirit, etc. Otherwise there is no use in reading it.

You must not understand the word law here in human fashion, i.e., a regulation about what sort of works must be done or must not be done. That's the way it is with human laws: you satisfy the demands of the law with works, whether your heart is in it or not. God judges what is in the depths of the heart. Therefore his law also makes demands on the depths of the heart and doesn't let the heart rest content in works; rather it punishes as hypocrisy and lies all works done apart from the depths of the heart. All human beings are called liars (Psalm 116), since none of them keeps or can keep God's law from the depths of the heart. Everyone finds inside himself an aversion to good and a craving for evil. Where there is no free desire for good, there the heart has not set itself on God's law. There also sin is surely to be found and the deserved wrath of God, whether a lot of good works and an honourable life appear outwardly or not.

Therefore in chapter 2, St Paul adds that the Jews are all sinners and says that only the doers of the law are justified in the sight of God. What he is saying is that no one is a doer of the law by works. On the contrary, he says to them, 'You teach that one should not commit adultery, and you commit adultery. You judge another in a certain matter and condemn yourselves in that same matter, because you do the very same thing that you judged in another.' It is as if he were saying, 'Outwardly you live quite properly in the works of the law and judge those who do not live the same way; you know how to teach everybody. You see the speck in another's eye but do not notice the beam in your own.'

Outwardly you keep the law with works out of fear of punishment or love of gain. Likewise you do everything without free desire and love of the law; you act out of aversion and force. You'd rather act otherwise if the law didn't exist. It follows, then, that you, in the depths of your heart, are an enemy of the law. What do you mean, therefore, by teaching another not to steal, when you, in the depths of your heart, are a thief and would be one outwardly too, if you dared. (Of course, outward work doesn't last long with such hypocrites.) So then, you teach others but not yourself; you don't even know what you are teaching. You've never understood the law rightly. Furthermore, the law increases sin, as St Paul says in chapter 5. That is because a person becomes more and more an enemy of the law the more it demands of him what he can't possibly do.

In chapter 7, St Paul says, 'The law is spiritual.' What does that mean? If the law were physical, then it could be satisfied by works, but since it is spiritual, no one can satisfy it unless everything he does springs from the depths of the heart. But no one can give such a heart except the Spirit of God, who makes the person be like the law, so that he actually conceives a heartfelt longing for the law and henceforward does everything, not through fear or coercion, but from a free heart. Such a law is spiritual since it can only be loved and fulfilled by such a heart and such a spirit. If the Spirit is not in the heart, then there remain sin, aversion and enmity against the law, which in itself is good, just and holy.

You must get used to the idea that it is one thing to do the works of the law and quite another to fulfill it. The works of the law are every thing that a person does or can do of his own free will and by his own powers to obey the law. But because in doing such works the heart abhors the law and yet is forced to obey it, the works are a total loss and are completely useless. That is what St Paul means in chapter 3 when he says, 'No human being is justified before God through the works of the law.' From this you can see that the scholastic theologians and sophists are seducers when they teach that you can prepare yourself for grace by means of works. How can anybody prepare himself for good by means of works if he does no good work except with aversion and constraint in his heart? How can such a work please God, if it proceeds from an averse and unwilling heart?

But to fulfill the law means to do its work eagerly, lovingly and freely, without the constraint of the law; it means to live well and in a manner pleasing to God, as though there were no law or punishment. It is the Holy Spirit, however, who puts such eagerness of unconstrained love into the heart, as Paul says in chapter 5. But the Spirit is given only in, with, and through faith in Jesus Christ, as Paul says in his introduction. So, too, faith comes only through the word of God, the Gospel, that preaches Christ: how he is both Son of God and man, how he died and rose for our sake. Paul says all this in chapters 3, 4 and 10.

That is why faith alone makes someone just and fulfills the law; faith it is that brings the Holy Spirit through the merits of Christ. The Spirit, in turn, renders the heart glad and free, as the law demands. Then good works proceed from faith itself. That is what Paul means in chapter 3 when, after he has thrown out the works of the law, he sounds as though he wants to abolish the law by faith. No, he says, we uphold the law through faith, i.e. we fulfill it through faith.

Sin in the Scriptures means not only external works of the body but also all those movements within us which bestir themselves and move us to do the external works, namely, the depth of the heart with all its powers. Therefore the word do should refer to a person's completely falling into sin. No external work of sin happens, after all, unless a person commit himself to it completely, body and soul. In particular, the Scriptures see into the heart, to the root and main source of all sin: unbelief in the depth of the heart. Thus, even as faith alone makes just and brings the Spirit and the desire to do good external works, so it is only unbelief which sins and exalts the flesh and brings desire to do evil external works. That's what happened to Adam and Eve in Paradise (cf. Genesis 3).

That is why only unbelief is called sin by Christ, as he says in John, chapter 16, 'The Spirit will punish the world because of sin, because it does not believe in me.' Furthermore, before good or bad works happen, which are the good or bad fruits of the heart, there has to be present in the heart either faith or unbelief, the root, sap and chief power of all sin. That is why, in the Scriptures, unbelief is called the head of the serpent and of the ancient dragon which the offspring of the woman, i.e. Christ, must crush, as was promised to Adam (cf. Genesis 3). Grace and gift differ in that grace actually denotes God's kindness or favour which he has towards us and by which he is disposed to pour Christ and the Spirit with his gifts into us, as becomes clear from chapter 5, where Paul says, 'Grace and gift are in Christ, etc.' The gifts and the Spirit increase daily in us, yet they are not complete, since evil desires and sins remain in us which war against the Spirit, as Paul says in chapter 7, and in Galatians, chapter 5. And Genesis, chapter 3, proclaims the enmity between the offspring of the woman and that of the serpent. But grace does do this much: that we are accounted completely just before God. God's grace is not divided into bits and pieces, as are the gifts, but grace takes us up completely into God's favour for the sake of Christ, our intercessor and mediator, so that the gifts may begin their work in us.

In this way, then, you should understand chapter 7, where St Paul portrays himself as still a sinner, while in chapter 8 he says that, because of the incomplete gifts and because of the Spirit, there is nothing damnable in those who are in Christ. Because our flesh has not been killed, we are still sinners, but because we believe in Christ and have the beginnings of the Spirit, God so shows us his favour and mercy, that he neither notices nor judges such sins. Rather he deals with us according to our belief in Christ until sin is killed.

Faith is not that human illusion and dream that some people think it is. When they hear and talk a lot about faith and yet see that no moral improvement and no good works result from it, they fall into error and say, 'Faith is not enough. You must do works if you want to be virtuous and get to heaven.' The result is that, when they hear the Gospel, they stumble and make for themselves with their own powers a concept in their hearts which says, 'I believe.' This concept they hold to be true faith. But since it is a human fabrication and thought and not an experience of the heart, it accomplishes nothing, and there follows no improvement.

Faith is a work of God in us, which changes us and brings us to birth anew from God (cf. John 1). It kills the old Adam, makes us completely different people in heart, mind, senses, and all our powers, and brings the Holy Spirit with it. What a living, creative, active powerful thing is faith! It is impossible that faith will ever stop doing good. Faith doesn't ask whether good works are to be done, but, before it is asked, it has done them. It is always active. Whoever doesn't do such works is without faith; he gropes and searches about him for faith and good works but doesn't know what faith or good works are. Even so, he chatters on with a great many words about faith and good works.

Faith is a living, unshakeable confidence in God's grace; it is so certain, that someone would die a thousand times for it. This kind of trust in and knowledge of God's grace makes a person joyful, confident, and happy with regard to God and all creatures. This is what the Holy Spirit does by faith. Through faith, a person will do good to everyone without coercion, willingly and happily; he will serve everyone, suffer everything for the love and praise of God, who has shown him such grace. It is as impossible to separate works from faith as burning and shining from fire. Therefore be on guard against your own false ideas and against the chatterers who think they are clever enough to make judgements about faith and good works but who are in reality the biggest fools. Ask God to work faith in you; otherwise you will remain eternally without faith, no matter what you try to do or fabricate.

Now justice is just such a faith. It is called God's justice or that justice which is valid in God's sight, because it is God who gives it and reckons it as justice for the sake of Christ our Mediator. It influences a person to give to everyone what he owes him. Through faith a person becomes sinless and eager for God's commands. Thus he gives God the honour due him and pays him what he owes him. He serves people willingly with the means available to him. In this way he pays everyone his due. Neither nature nor free will nor our own powers can bring about such a justice, for even as no one can give himself faith, so too he cannot remove unbelief. How can he then take away even the smallest sin? Therefore everything which takes place outside faith or in unbelief is lie, hypocrisy and sin (Romans 14), no matter how smoothly it may seem to go.

You must not understand flesh here as denoting only unchastity or spirit as denoting only the inner heart. Here St Paul calls flesh (as does Christ in John 3) everything born of flesh, i.e. the whole human being with body and soul, reason and senses, since everything in him tends towards the flesh. That is why you should know enough to call that person 'fleshly' who, without grace, fabricates, teaches and chatters about high spiritual matters. You can learn the same thing from Galatians, chapter 5, where St Paul calls heresy and hatred works of the flesh. And in Romans, chapter 8, he says that, through the flesh, the law is weakened. He says this, not of unchastity, but of all sins, most of all of unbelief, which is the most spiritual of vices.

On the other hand, you should know enough to call that person 'spiritual' who is occupied with the most outward of works as was Christ, when he washed the feet of the disciples, and Peter, when he steered his boat and fished. So then, a person is 'flesh' who, inwardly and outwardly, lives only to do those things which are of use to the flesh and to temporal existence. A person is 'spirit' who, inwardly and outwardly, lives only to do those things which are of use to the spirit and to the life to come.

Unless you understand these words in this way, you will never understand either this letter of St Paul or any book of the Scriptures. Be on guard, therefore, against any teacher who uses these words differently, no matter who he be, whether Jerome, Augustine, Ambrose, Origen or anyone else as great as or greater than they. Now let us turn to the letter itself.

The first duty of a preacher of the Gospel is, through his revealing of the law and of sin, to rebuke and to turn into sin everything in life that does not have the Spirit and faith in Christ as its base. Thereby he will lead people to a recognition of their miserable condition, and thus they will become humble and yearn for help. This is what St Paul does. He begins in chapter 1 by rebuking the gross sins and unbelief which are in plain view, as were (and still are) the sins of the pagans, who live without God's grace. He says that, through the Gospel, God is revealing his wrath from heaven upon all mankind because of the godless and unjust lives they live. For, although they know and recognize day by day that there is a God, yet human nature in itself, without grace, is so evil that it neither thanks nor honours God. This nature blinds itself and continually falls into wickedness, even going so far as to commit idolatry and other horrible sins and vices. It is unashamed of itself and leaves such things unpunished in others.

In chapter 2, St Paul extends his rebuke to those who appear outwardly pious or who sin secretly. Such were the Jews, and such are all hypocrites still, who live virtuous lives but without eagerness and love; in their heart they are enemies of God's law and like to judge other people. That's the way with hypocrites: they think that they are pure but are actually full of greed, hate, pride and all sorts of filth (cf. Matthew 23). These are they who despise God's goodness and, by their hardness of heart, heap wrath upon themselves. Thus Paul explains the law rightly when he lets no one remain without sin but proclaims the wrath of God to all who want to live virtuously by nature or by free will. He makes them out to be no better than public sinners; he says they are hard of heart and unrepentant.

In chapter 3, Paul lumps both secret and public sinners together: the one, he says, is like the other; all are sinners in the sight of God. Besides, the Jews had God's word, even though many did not believe in it. But still God's truth and faith in him are not thereby rendered useless. St Paul introduces, as an aside, the saying from Psalm 51, that God remains true to his words. Then he returns to his topic and proves from Scripture that they are all sinners and that no one becomes just through the works of the law but that God gave the law only so that sin might be perceived.

Next St Paul teaches the right way to be virtuous and to be saved; he says that they are all sinners, unable to glory in God. They must, however, be justified through faith in Christ, who has merited this for us by his blood and has become for us a mercy seat [cf. Exodus 25:17; Leviticus 16:14ff; and John 2:2] in the presence of God, who forgives us all our previous sins. In so doing, God proves that it is his justice alone, which he gives through faith, that helps us, the justice which was at the appointed time revealed through the Gospel and, previous to that, was witnessed to by the Law and the Prophets. Therefore the law is set up by faith, but the works of the law, along with the glory taken in them, are knocked down by faith.

In chapters 1 to 3, St Paul has revealed sin for what it is and has taught the way of faith which leads to justice. Now in chapter 4 he deals with some objections and criticisms. He takes up first the one that people raise who, on hearing that faith makes just without works, say, 'What? Shouldn't we do any good works?' Here St Paul holds up Abraham as an example. He says, 'What did Abraham accomplish with his good works? Were they all good for nothing and useless?' He concludes that Abraham was made righteous apart from all his works by faith alone. Even before the 'work' of his circumcision, Scripture praises him as being just on account of faith alone (cf. Genesis 15). Now if the work of his circumcision did nothing to make him just, a work that God had commanded him to do and hence a work of obedience, then surely no other good work can do anything to make a person just. Even as Abraham's circumcision was an outward sign with which he proved his justice based on faith, so too all good works are only outward signs which flow from faith and are the fruits of faith; they prove that the person is already inwardly just in the sight of God.

St Paul verifies his teaching on faith in chapter 3 with a powerful example from Scripture. He calls as witness David, who says in Psalm 32 that a person becomes just without works but doesn't remain without works once he has become just. Then Paul extends this example and applies it against all other works of the law. He concludes that the Jews cannot be Abraham's heirs just because of their blood relationship to him and still less because of the works of the law. Rather, they have to inherit

Abrahams's faith if they want to be his real heirs, since it was prior to the Law of Moses and the law of circumcision that Abraham became just through faith and was called a father of all believers. St Paul adds that the law brings about more wrath than grace, because no one obeys it with love and eagerness. More disgrace than grace comes from the works of the law. Therefore faith alone can obtain the grace promised to Abraham. Examples like these are written for our sake, that we also should have faith.

In chapter 5, St Paul comes to the fruits and works of faith, namely: joy, peace, love for God and for all people; in addition: assurance, steadfastness, confidence, courage, and hope in sorrow and suffering. All of these follow where faith is genuine, because of the overflowing good will that God has shown in Christ: he had him die for us before we could ask him for it, yes, even while we were still his enemies. Thus we have established that faith, without any good works, makes just. It does not follow from that, however, that we should not do good works; rather it means that morally upright works do not remain lacking. About such works the 'works-holy' people know nothing; they invent for themselves their own works in which are neither peace nor joy nor assurance nor love nor hope nor steadfastness nor any kind of genuine Christian works or faith.

Next St Paul makes a digression, a pleasant little side-trip, and relates where both sin and justice, death and life come from. He opposes these two: Adam and Christ. What he wants to say is that Christ, a second Adam, had to come in order to make us heirs of his justice through a new spiritual birth in faith, just as the old Adam made us heirs of sin through the old fleshy birth.

St Paul proves, by this reasoning, that a person cannot help himself by his works to get from sin to justice any more than he can prevent his own physical birth. St Paul also proves that the divine law, which should have been well-suited, if anything was, for helping people to obtain justice, not only was no help at all when it did come, but it even increased sin. Evil human nature, consequently, becomes more hostile to it; the more the law forbids it to indulge its own desires, the more it wants to. Thus the law makes Christ all the more necessary and demands more grace to help human nature.

In chapter 6, St Paul takes up the special work of faith, the struggle which the spirit wages against the flesh to kill off those sins and desires that remain after a person has been made just. He teaches us that faith doesn't so free us from sin that we can be idle, lazy and self-assured, as though there were no more sin in us. Sin is there, but, because of faith that struggles against it, God does not reckon sin as deserving damnation. Therefore we have in our own selves a lifetime of work cut out for us; we have to tame our body, kill its lusts, force its members to obey the spirit and not the lusts. We must do this so that we may conform to the death and resurrection of Christ and complete our Baptism, which signifies a death to sin and a new life of grace. Our aim is to be completely clean from sin and then to rise bodily with Christ and live forever.

St Paul says that we can accomplish all this because we are in grace and not in the law. He explains that to be 'outside the law' is not the same as having no law and being able to do what you please. No, being 'under the law' means living without grace, surrounded by the works of the law. Then surely sin reigns by means of the law, since no one is naturally well-disposed towards the law. That very condition, however, is the greatest sin. But grace makes the law lovable to us, so there is then no sin any more, and the law is no longer against us but one with us.

This is true freedom from sin and from the law; St Paul writes about this for the rest of the chapter. He says it is a freedom only to do good with eagerness and to live a good life without the coercion of the law. This freedom is, therefore, a spiritual freedom which does not suspend the law but which supplies what the law demands, namely eagerness and love. These silence the law so that it has no further cause to drive people on and make demands of them. It's as though you owed something to a moneylender and couldn't pay him. You could be rid of him in one of two ways: either he would take nothing from you and would tear up his account book, or a pious man would pay for you and give you what you needed to satisfy your debt. That's exactly how Christ freed us from the law. Therefore our freedom is not a wild, fleshy freedom that has no obligation to do anything. On the contrary, it is a freedom that does a great deal, indeed everything, yet is free of the law's demands and debts.

In chapter 7, St Paul confirms the foregoing by an analogy drawn from married life. When a man dies, the wife is free; the one is free and clear of the other. It is not the case that the woman may not or should not marry another man; rather she is now for the first time free to marry someone else. She could not do this before she was free of her first husband. In the same way, our conscience is bound to the law so long as our condition is that of the sinful old man. But when the old man is killed by the spirit, then the conscience is free, and conscience and law are quit of each other. Not that conscience should now do nothing; rather, it should now for the first time truly cling to its second husband, Christ, and bring forth the fruit of life.

Next St Paul sketches further the nature of sin and the law. It is the law that makes sin really active and powerful, because the old man gets more and more hostile to the law since he can't pay the debt demanded by the law. Sin is his very nature; of himself he can't do otherwise. And so the law is his death and torture. Now the law is not itself evil; it is our evil nature that cannot tolerate that the good law should demand good from it. It's like the case of a sick person, who cannot tolerate that you demand that he run and jump around and do other things that a healthy person does.

St Paul concludes here that, if we understand the law properly and comprehend it in the best possible way, then we will see that its sole function is to remind us of our sins, to kill us by our sins, and to make us deserving of eternal wrath. Conscience learns and experiences all this in detail when it comes face to face with the law. It follows, then, that we must have something else, over and above the law, which can make a person virtuous and cause him to be saved. Those, however, who do not understand the law rightly are blind; they go their way boldly and think they are satisfying the law with works. They don't know how much the law demands, namely, a free, willing, eager heart. That is the reason that they don't see Moses rightly before their eyes. For them he is covered and concealed by the veil.

Then St Paul shows how spirit and flesh struggle with each other in one person. He gives himself as an example, so that we may learn how to kill sin in ourselves. He gives both spirit and flesh the name 'law', so that, just as it is in the nature of divine law to drive a person on and make demands of him, so too the flesh drives and demands and rages against the spirit and wants to have its own way. Likewise the spirit drives and demands against the flesh and wants to have its own way. This feud lasts in us for as long as we live, in one person more, in another less, depending on whether spirit or flesh is stronger. Yet the whole human being is both: spirit and flesh. The human being fights with himself until he becomes completely spiritual.

In chapter 8, St Paul comforts fighters such as these and tells them that this flesh will not bring them condemnation. He goes on to show what the nature of flesh and spirit are. Spirit, he says, comes from Christ, who has given us his Holy Spirit; the Holy

Spirit makes us spiritual and restrains the flesh. The Holy Spirit assures us that we are God's children no matter how furiously sin may rage within us, so long as we follow the Spirit and struggle against sin in order to kill it. Because nothing is so effective in deadening the flesh as the cross and suffering, Paul comforts us in our suffering. He says that the Spirit, love and all creatures will stand by us; the Spirit in us groans and all creatures long with us that we be freed from the flesh and from sin. Thus we see that these three chapters, 6, 7 and 8, all deal with the one work of faith, which is to kill the old Adam and to constrain the flesh.

In chapters 9, 10 and 11, St Paul teaches us about the eternal providence of God. It is the original source which determines who would believe and who wouldn't, who can be set free from sin and who cannot. Such matters have been taken out of our hands and are put into God's hands so that we might become virtuous. It is absolutely necessary that it be so, for we are so weak and unsure of ourselves that, if it depended on us, no human being would be saved. The devil would overpower all of us. But God is steadfast; his providence will not fail, and no one can prevent its realization. Therefore we have hope against sin.

But here we must shut the mouths of those sacrilegious and arrogant spirits who, mere beginners that they are, bring their reason to bear on this matter and commence, from their exalted position, to probe the abyss of divine providence and uselessly trouble themselves about whether they are predestined or not. These people must surely plunge to their ruin, since they will either despair or abandon themselves to a life of chance.

You, however, follow the reasoning of this letter in the order in which it is presented. Fix your attention first of all on Christ and the Gospel, so that you may recognize your sin and his grace. Then struggle against sin, as chapters 1–8 have taught you to. Finally, when you have come, in chapter 8, under the shadow of the cross and suffering, they will teach you, in chapters 9–11, about providence and what a comfort it is. Apart from suffering, the cross and the pangs of death, you cannot come to grips with providence without harm to yourself and secret anger against God. The old Adam must be quite dead before you can endure this matter and drink this strong wine. Therefore make sure you don't drink wine while you are still a babe at the breast. There is a proper measure, time and age for understanding every doctrine.

In chapter 12, St Paul teaches the true liturgy and makes all Christians priests, so that they may offer, not money or cattle, as priests do in the Law, but their own bodies, by putting their desires to death. Next he describes the outward conduct of Christians whose lives are governed by the Spirit; he tells how they teach, preach, rule, serve, give, suffer, love, live and act towards friend, foe and everyone. These are the works that a Christian does, for, as I have said, faith is not idle.

In chapter 13, St Paul teaches that one should honour and obey the secular authorities. He includes this, not because it makes people virtuous in the sight of God, but because it does insure that the virtuous have outward peace and protection and that the wicked cannot do evil without fear and in undisturbed peace. Therefore it is the duty of virtuous people to honour secular authority, even though they do not, strictly speaking, need it. Finally, St Paul sums up everything in love and gathers it all into the example of Christ: what he has done for us, we must also do and follow after him.

In chapter 14, St Paul teaches that one should carefully guide those with weak conscience and spare them. One shouldn't use Christian freedom to harm but rather to help the weak. Where that isn't done, there follow dissension and despising of the Gospel, on which everything else depends. It is better to give way a little to the weak in faith until they become stronger than to have the teaching of the Gospel perish completely. This work is a particularly necessary work of love especially now when people, by eating meat and by other freedoms, are brashly, boldly and unnecessarily shaking weak consciences which have not yet come to know the truth.

In chapter 15, St Paul cites Christ as an example to show that we must also have patience with the weak, even those who fail by sinning publicly or by their disgusting morals. We must not cast them aside but must bear with them until they become better. That is the way Christ treated us and still treats us every day; he puts up with our vices, our wicked morals and all our imperfection, and he helps us ceaselessly. Finally Paul prays for the Christians at Rome; he praises them and commends them to God. He points out his own office and the message that he preaches. He makes an unobtrusive plea for a contribution for the poor in Jerusalem. Unalloyed love is the basis of all he says and does.

The last chapter consists of greetings. But Paul also includes a salutary warning against human doctrines which are preached alongside the Gospel and which do a great deal of harm. It's as though he had clearly seen that out of Rome and through the Romans would come the deceitful, harmful Canons along with the entire brood and swarm of human laws and commands that is now drowning the whole world and has blotted out this letter and the whole of the Scriptures, along with the Spirit and faith. Nothing remains but the idol Belly, and St Paul depicts those people here as its servants. God deliver us from them. Amen.

We find in this letter, then, the richest possible teaching about what a Christian should know: the meaning of law, Gospel, sin, punishment, grace, faith, justice, Christ, God, good works, love, hope and the cross. We learn how we are to act towards everyone, towards the virtuous and sinful, towards the strong and the weak, friend and foe, and towards ourselves. Paul bases everything firmly on Scripture and proves his points with examples from his own experience and from the Prophets, so that nothing more could be desired. Therefore it seems that St Paul, in writing this letter, wanted to compose a summary of the whole of Christian and evangelical teaching which would also be an introduction to the whole Old Testament. Without doubt, whoever takes this letter to heart possesses the light and power of the Old Testament. Therefore each and every Christian should make this letter the habitual and constant object of his study. God grant us his grace to do so. Amen.

Psalm 19

C.H. SPURGEON, THE TREASURY OF DAVID

Verse 1. 'The heavens declare the glory of God.'

⌘ The book of nature has three leaves, heaven, earth, and sea, of which heaven is the first and the most glorious, and by its aid we are able to see the beauties of the other two. Any book without its first page would be sadly imperfect, and especially the great Natural Bible, since its first pages, the sun, moon, and stars, supply light to the rest of the volume, and are thus the keys, without which the writing which follows would be dark and undiscerned. Man walking erect was evidently made to scan the skies, and he who begins to read creation by studying the stars begins the book at the right place.

The heavens are plural for their variety, comprising the watery heavens with their clouds of countless forms, the aerial heavens with their calms and tempests, the solar heavens with all the glories of the day, and the starry heavens with all the marvels of the night; what the Heaven of heavens must be hath not entered into the heart of man, but there in chief all things are telling the glory of God. Any part of creation has more instruction in it than human mind will ever exhaust, but the celestial realm is peculiarly rich in spiritual lore. The heavens declare, or are declaring, for the continuance of their testimony is intended by the participles employed; every moment God's existence, power, wisdom and goodness, are being sounded abroad by the heavenly heralds which shine upon us from above. He who would guess at divine sublimity should gaze upward into the starry vault; he who would imagine infinity must peer into the boundless expanse; he who desires to see divine wisdom should consider the balancing of the orbs; he who would know divine fidelity must mark the regularity of the planetary motions; and he who would attain some conceptions of divine power, greatness, and majesty, must estimate the forces of attraction, the magnitude of the fixed stars, and the brightness of the whole celestial train. It is not merely glory that the heavens declare, but the 'glory of God', for they deliver to us such unanswerable arguments for a conscious, intelligent, planning, controlling, and presiding Creator, that no unprejudiced person can remain unconvinced by them. The testimony given by the heavens is no mere hint, but a plain, unmistakable declaration; and it is a declaration of the most constant and abiding kind. Yet for all this, to what avail is the loudest declaration to a deaf man, or the clearest showing to one spiritually blind? God the Holy Ghost must illuminate us, or all the suns in the milky way never will.

'The firmament sheweth his handywork'; not handy in the vulgar use of that term, but handwork. The expanse is full of the works of the Lord's skilful, creating hands; hands being attributed to the great creating Spirit to set forth his care and workmanlike action, and to meet the poor comprehension of mortals. It is humbling to find that even when the most devout and elevated minds are desirous to express their loftiest thoughts of God, they must use words and metaphors drawn from the earth. We are children, and must each confess, 'I think as a child, I speak as a child.' In the expanse above us God flies, as it were, his starry flag to show that the King is at home, and hangs out his escutcheon that atheists may see how he despises their denunciations of him. He who looks up to the firmament and then writes himself down an atheist, brands himself at the same moment as an idiot or a liar. Strange is it that some who love God are yet afraid to study the God-declaring book of nature; the mock-spirituality of some believers, who are too heavenly to consider the heavens, has given colour to the vaunts of infidels that nature contradicts revelation. The wisest of men are those who with pious eagerness trace the goings forth of Jehovah as well in creation as in grace; only the foolish have any fears lest the honest study of the one should injure our faith in the other. Dr M'Cosh has well said, 'We have often mourned over the attempts made to set the works of God against the Word of God, and thereby excite, propagate, and perpetuate jealousies fitted to separate parties that ought to live in closest union. In particular, we have always regretted that endeavours should have been made to depreciate nature with a view of exalting revelation; it has always appeared to us to be nothing else than the degrading of one part of God's work in the hope thereby of exalting and recommending another. Let not science and religion be reckoned as opposing citadels, frowning defiance upon each other, and their troops brandishing their armour in hostile attitude. They have too many common foes, if they would but think of it, in ignorance and prejudice, in passion and vice, under all their forms, to admit of their lawfully wasting their strength in a useless warfare with each other. Science has a foundation, and so has religion; let them unite their foundations, and the basis will be broader, and they will be two compartments of one great fabric reared to the glory of God. Let one be the outer and the other the inner court. In the one, let all look, and admire and adore; and in the other, let those who have faith kneel, and pray, and praise. Let the one be the sanctuary where human learning may present its richest incense as an offering to God, and the other the holiest of all, separated from it by a veil now rent in twain, and in which, on a blood-sprinkled mercy-seat, we pour out the love of a reconciled heart, and hear the oracles of the living God.'

LETTERS

❧◦❧

The hope of heaven

ANSELM, *LETTERS*

To Ernest, Bishop of Rochester (1076)

When I learn that your body is worn out by fierce and incessant pain that brings you almost to the point of death, the news saddens me and humanly speaking fills me with grief. However, the thought that this is precisely the way your soul is being made ripe for eternity refreshes me and I watch your growth in holiness with spiritual happiness.

Your reverence is surely well aware that afflictions and the suffering of the body burn away the rust of sin and perfect the life of the just. Holy Scripture assures us that God scourges every son whom he receives (see Hebrews 12:6); it tells us further that tribulation brings endurance, and endurance brings character, and character brings hope, and hope does not disappoint us (see Romans 5:3–4).

This teaches us beyond all doubt that we will find joy in suffering in proportion as we have lived in hope and as we have laboured for the perfection of our inheritance as sons of God.

Experiencing God

JOHN NEWTON, *CARDIPHONIA*

My Dear Miss M.,

You say: 'It never came with power and life to my soul, that he died for me.' If you mean, you never had any extraordinary sudden manifestation, something like a vision or voice from heaven, confirming it to you, I can say the same. But I know he died for sinners; I know I am a sinner; I know he invites those who are ready to perish; I am such a one; I know, upon his own invitation, that he has been with me until now, otherwise I should have been an apostate long ago; and therefore I know that he died for me; for had he been pleased to kill me (as he justly might have done), he would not have shown me such things as these.

If I must perish, would the Lord
Have taught my heart to love his word?
Would he have giv'n me eyes to see
My danger and my remedy?
Reveal'd his name, and bid me pray,
Had he resolv'd to say me nay?

I know that I am a child, because he teaches me to say – Abba, Father. I know that I am his, because he has enabled me to choose him for mine; for such a choice and desire never could have taken place in my heart, if he had not placed it there himself. The love I bear him is but a faint and feeble spark, but it is an emanation from himself: he kindled it, and he keeps it alive; and because it is his work, I trust many waters shall not quench it.

By God's grace

JOHN NEWTON, *CARDIPHONIA*

Letter to Mr B. (May 10, 1775)

My Dear Sir,

I hope you will find the Lord present at all times, and in all places. When it is so, we are at home everywhere; when it is otherwise, home is a prison, and abroad a wilderness. I know what I ought to desire, and what I do desire. I point him out to others as the all in all; I esteem him as such in my own judgement; but, alas, my experience abounds with complaints.

He is my sun; but clouds, and sometimes walls, intercept him from my view. He is my strength; yet I am prone to lean upon reeds. He is my friend; but on my part there is such coldness and ingratitude, as no other friend could bear. But still he is gracious and shames me with his repeated multiplied goodness.

O for a warmer heart, a more active zeal, a greater deliverance from the effects of this body of sin and death! However, though I cannot say I labour more abundantly than they all, I have reason to say with gratitude: 'by the grace of God I am what I am.' My poor story would be much worse, did not he support, restrain, and watch over me every minute.

CONVERSION STORIES

❧❀❧

Augustine

AUGUSTINE, *CONFESSIONS*

❧I threw myself down under a fig tree and collapsed in tears…

'How long, O Lord, how long will you be angry? For ever? Do not hold against us our former sins' [cf. Psalm 79:5–8, 85:5] – for I felt I was bound by them … 'Tomorrow and tomorrow? Why not now? Why isn't there an end to my dirtiness here and now?'

I was talking like this and crying with most heartfelt bitterness when I heard a voice (perhaps a child's voice, I'm not sure) coming from a nearby house. It was chanting and repeating the words 'Pick it up and read it!' Immediately my face changed and I began seriously to wonder whether children used these words in any of their games, but I couldn't remember ever hearing anything like them. So, subduing my tears, I got up, thinking it must be nothing other than a command from God to open the book and read the first chapter I found. For I had heard that Antony, coming in during the reading of the Gospel, received what was being read as a warning to himself: 'Go, sell your possessions and give to the poor, and you will have treasure in heaven. Then come, follow me' (Matthew 19:21). And he was immediately converted to you by this message.

Then I ran back to where Alypius was sitting; for, when I left him, I had left the Apostle's book lying there. I picked it up, opened it, and silently read the passage (Romans 13:13–14). I first set eyes on: 'Let us behave decently, as in the daytime, not in orgies and drunkenness, not in sexual immorality and debauchery, not in dissension and jealousy. Rather, clothe yourselves with the Lord Jesus Christ, and do not think about how to gratify the desires of the sinful nature.' I didn't want to read any further, and it wasn't necessary. As I reached the end of the sentence, the light of peace seemed to shine on my heart, and every shadow of doubt disappeared.

Blaise Pascal

BLAISE PASCAL, *MEMORIAL*

[Converted in Rouen in 1646, Pascal had a 'second conversion' on 23 November 1654, a spiritual revival encountering the Holy Spirit that lasted from 10.30 p.m. to 12.30 a.m. He recorded this on parchment in a 'Memorial' which he sewed into the lining of his doublet, keeping it with him to his death.]

The Memorial
In the Year of Grace 1654,
On Monday, 23 November, Feast of Saint Clement,
Pope and Martyr,
and of others in the Martyrology,
and Eve of Saint Chrysogonus and other Martyrs,
From about half past ten at night until about half past twelve.

Fire
'God of Abraham, God of Isaac, God of Jacob' (Exodus 6:3),
not of the philosophers and scientists.
Certitude. Certitude. Feeling. Joy. Peace.
God of Jesus Christ.
God of Jesus Christ.

'My God and your God' (John 20:17).

'You shall be my God' (Ruth 1:16).
Forgetting the world and all things, except only God.
He is to be found only by the ways taught in the Gospel.
Greatness of the human soul.
'Righteous Father, the world has not known Thee, but I have
known Thee'
(John 17:25).
Joy, joy, joy, tears of joy.
I have fallen away from Him.
'They have forsaken me, the fountain of living water'
(Jeremiah 2:13).
'My God, wilt thou forsake me?' (see Matthew 27:46).
May I not be separated from Him in all eternity.
'Now this is eternal life, that they may know Thee, the only
true God, and Jesus Christ, whom Thou hast sent' (John 17:3).
Jesus Christ.
Jesus Christ.
I have fallen away from Him; I have fled from Him, denied
Him, crucified Him.
May I not be separated from Him for eternity.
We hold Him only by the ways taught in the Gospel.
Renunciation total and sweet.
Total submission to Jesus Christ and to my director.

Eternally in joy for one day of trial upon earth.
'I will not forget thy Word' (Psalm 119:16). Amen.

John Bunyan

JOHN BROWN, *JOHN BUNYAN*

A voice did suddenly dart from heaven into my soul

❧ There are some natures to whom the great spiritual world of the unseen is always present as the background of life. It was so with Shakespeare. It was so also with Bunyan, though in a different way. Even when he was a child, the wrong things of the day were followed by the remorse, and fears, and dread dreams of the night. But the real struggle began later, when after his marriage and the reading of his wife's books, he was seen 'going to church twice a day, and with the foremost'. He had not done this long before there arose a fight with his conscience about Sunday sports, in the course of which there came the weird voices that seemed to be shouted into his ear on Elstow Green.

Somewhere on the sward round the broken pillar of the old Market Cross he was one Sunday in the middle of a game of cat [a forerunner of cricket]. He had struck it one blow from the hole and was about to strike it the second time, when, as he says, 'A voice did suddenly dart from heaven into my soul, which said, Wilt thou leave thy sins and go to heaven, or have thy sins and go to hell? At this I was put to an exceeding maze.

'Wherefore, leaving my cat upon the ground, I looked up to heaven, and was as if I had with the eyes of my understanding, seen the Lord Jesus looking down upon me, as being very hotly displeased with me.'

Thus conscience-stricken he afterwards made a desperate fling to be rid of conscience altogether, only to find, as other men have, that its grip was tighter than he thought...

His wonderful power of dreaming waking dreams

✌Then blossomed into shape his wonderful power of dreaming waking dreams. There were these good people at Bedford sitting on the sunny side of a mountain, while he was separated from them by a wall all about, and shivering in the cold. Round and round that wall he goes to see if there be no opening, be it ever so narrow, and at last he finds one. But it is narrow, indeed so narrow that none can get through but those who are in downright earnest, and who leave the wicked world behind them. There is just room for body and soul, but not for body and soul and sin. It must be a strait gate through which a man gets rid of self; but by dint of sidling and striving he first gets in his head, then his shoulders, and then his whole body, at which he is exceeding glad, for now too he is in the sunshine and is comforted. But as yet this is only in a dream, and dreams tarry not...

Methought I saw with the eye of my soul, Jesus Christ at God's right hand

✌One day as he was passing into the field, still with some fears in his heart, suddenly this sentence fell into his soul, 'Thy righteousness is in heaven': and methought withal I saw with the eye of my soul, Jesus Christ at God's right hand. I saw, moreover, that it was not my good frame of heart that made my righteousness better, nor yet my bad frame that made my righteousness worse; for my righteousness was Jesus Christ Himself, the same yesterday, today, and for ever. Now did my chains fall from my legs indeed; I was loosed from my afflictions and irons. Oh, methought, Christ! Christ! there was nothing but Christ that was before my eyes! I could look from myself to Him and should reckon that all those graces of God that now were green on me, were yet like those crack-groats and fourpence halfpennies that rich men carry in their purses, when their gold is in their trunks at home! Oh, I saw my gold was in my trunk at home! In Christ my Lord and Saviour! Now Christ was all; all my wisdom, all my righteousness, all my sanctification, and all my redemption!'

John Wesley

JOHN WESLEY, *JOURNAL*, ENTRY FOR 24 MAY 1738
✒About a quarter before nine, while he [the preacher at Aldersgate Street Chapel] was describing the change which God works in the heart through faith in Christ, I felt I did trust in Christ, Christ alone, for salvation, and an assurance was given me that he had taken away my sins, even mine, and saved me from the law of sin and death.

John Newton

JOHN NEWTON, *AN AUTHENTIC NARRATIVE OF SOME REMARKABLE AND INTERESTING PARTICULARS IN THE LIFE OF —[JOHN NEWTON], IN FOURTEEN LETTERS*
✒[On his way home in 1748 Newton spent a night on a waterlogged boat, with death staring him in the face, but found that this was the moment when God spoke to his conscience. Later Newton referred to this time as the 'Great Deliverance'.]

I went to bed that night in my usual security and indifference; but was awakened from a sound sleep by the force of a violent sea, which broke on board us. The sea had torn away the upper timbers on one side, and made the ship a mere wreck in a few minutes. Taking in all the circumstances, it was astonishing, and almost miraculous, that any of us survived to relate the story. We had immediate recourse to the pumps; but the water increased against all our efforts: some of us were set to bailing in another part of the vessel, that is, to lade it out with buckets and pails. I continued doing this till noon, with almost every passing wave breaking over my head; but we made ourselves fast with ropes, that we might not be washed away. Although I dreaded death now, I thought, if the Christian religion were true, I could not be forgiven.

The next day I began to pray. My prayer was like the cry of the ravens, which yet the Lord does not disdain to hear. I now began to think of that Jesus whom I had so often derided: I recollected the particulars of his life, and of his death; a death for sins not his own, but, as I remembered, for the sake of those who in their distress should put their trust in him. My companions in danger were either quite unaffected, or soon forgot it all: but it was not so with me; not that I was any wiser or better than they, but because the Lord was pleased to vouchsafe me peculiar mercy. I had a New Testament and was struck particularly by the Prodigal, Luke chapter 15. Before we arrived in Ireland I had a satisfactory evidence in my own mind of the truth of the Gospel, as considered in itself, and its exact suitableness to answer all my needs. I saw that, by the way there pointed out, God might declare, not his mercy only, but his justice also, in the pardon of sin, on the account of the obedience and sufferings of Jesus Christ. My judgement at that time embraced the sublime doctrine of 'God manifest in the flesh, reconciling the world to himself'.

JOURNALS, DIARIES, BIOGRAPHIES AND AUTOBIOGRAPHIES

A mother's tears

AUGUSTINE, *CONFESSIONS*

℘And Thou sentest Thine hand from above, and drewest my soul out of that profound darkness, my mother, Thy faithful one, weeping to Thee for me, more than mothers weep the bodily deaths of their children. For she, by that faith and spirit which she had from Thee, discerned the death wherein I lay, and Thou heardest her, O Lord; Thou heardest her, and despised not her tears, when streaming down, they watered the ground under her eyes in every place where she prayed; yea, Thou heardest her. For whence was that dream whereby Thou comforted her; so that she allowed me to live with her, and to eat at the same table in the house, which she had begun to shrink from, abhorring and detesting the blasphemies of my error? For she saw herself standing on a certain wooden rule, and a shining youth coming towards her, cheerful and smiling upon her, herself grieving, and overwhelmed with grief. But he having (in order to instruct, as is their wont, not to be instructed) enquired of her the causes of her grief and daily tears, and she answering that she was bewailing my perdition, he bade her rest contented, and told her to look and observe, 'That where she was, there was I also.' And when she looked, she saw me standing by her in the same rule. Whence was this, but that Thine ears were towards her heart? O Thou Good omnipotent, who so carest for every one of us, as if Thou caredst for him only; and so for all, as if they were but one!

Whence was this also, that when she had told me this vision, and I would fain bend it to mean, 'That she rather should not despair of being one day what I was'; she presently, without any hesitation, replies: 'No; for it was not told me that, "where he, there thou also"; but "where thou, there he also".' I confess to Thee, O Lord, that to the best of my remembrance (and I have oft spoken of this), that Thy answer, through my waking mother, – that she was not perplexed by the plausibility of my false interpretation, and so quickly saw what was to be seen, and which I certainly had not perceived before she spake, – even then moved me more than the dream itself, by which a joy to the holy woman, to be fulfilled so long after, was, for the consolation of her present anguish, so long before foreseen. For almost nine years passed, in which I wallowed in the mire of that deep pit, and the darkness of falsehood, often assaying to rise, but dashed down the more grievously. All which time that chaste, godly, and sober widow (such as Thou lovest), now more cheered with hope, yet no whit relaxing in her weeping and mourning, ceased not at all hours of her devotions to bewail my case unto Thee. And her prayers entered into Thy presence; and yet Thou sufferedst me to be yet involved and reinvolved in that darkness.

Thou gavest her meantime another answer, which I call to mind; for much I pass by, hasting to those things which more press me to confess unto Thee, and much I do not remember. Thou gavest her then another answer, by a Priest of Thine, a certain Bishop brought up in Thy Church, and well studied in Thy books. Whom when this woman had entreated to vouchsafe to converse with me, refute my errors, unteach me ill things, and teach me good things (for this he was wont to do, when he found persons fitted to receive it), he refused, wisely, as I afterwards perceived. For he answered, that I was yet unteachable, being puffed up with the novelty of that heresy, and had already perplexed divers unskilful persons with captious questions, as she had told him: 'but let him alone a while' (saith he), 'only pray God for him, he will of himself by reading find what that error is, and how great its impiety.' At the same time he told her, how himself, when a little one, had by his seduced mother been consigned over to the Manichees, and had not only read, but frequently copied out almost all, their books, and had (without any argument or proof from any one) seen how much that sect was to be avoided; and had avoided it. Which when he had said, and she would not be satisfied, but urged him more, with entreaties and many tears, that he would see me and discourse with me; he, a little displeased at her importunity, saith, 'Go thy ways and God bless thee, for it is not possible that the son of these tears should perish.' Which answer she took (as she often mentioned in her conversations with me) as if it had sounded from heaven.

A state of total privation

MADAME GUYON, *AUTOBIOGRAPHY*

⊸◎About this time I fell into a state of total privation which lasted nearly seven years. I seemed to myself cast down like Nebuchadnezzar, to live among beasts; a deplorable state, yet of the greatest advantage to me, by the use which divine wisdom made of it. This state of emptiness, darkness, and impotency, went far beyond any trials I had ever yet met. I have since experienced, that the prayer of the heart when it appears most dry and barren, nevertheless is not ineffectual nor offered in vain. God gives what is best for us, though not what we most relish or wish for. Were people but convinced of this truth, they would be far from complaining all their lives. By causing us death He would procure us life; for all our happiness, spiritual, temporal and eternal, consists in resigning ourselves to God, leaving it to Him to do in us and with us as He pleases, and with so much the more submission; as things please us less. By this pure dependence on His Spirit, everything is given us admirably. Our very weaknesses, in His hand, prove a source of humiliation. If the soul were faithful to leave itself in the hand of God, sustaining all His operations whether gratifying or mortifying, suffering itself to be conducted, from moment to moment, by His hand, and annihilated by the strokes of His Providence, without complaining, or desiring anything but what it has; it would soon arrive at the experience of the eternal truth, though it might not at once know the ways and methods by which God conducted it there.

People want to direct God instead of resigning themselves to be directed by Him. They want to show Him a way, instead of passively following that wherein He leads them. Hence many souls, called to enjoy God Himself, and not barely His gifts, spend all their lives in running after little consolations, and feeding on them – resting there only, making all their happiness to consist therein.

If my chains and my imprisonment in any way afflict you, I pray that they may serve to engage you to seek nothing but God for Himself alone, and never to desire to possess Him but by the death of your whole selves, never to seek to be something in the ways of the Spirit, but choose to enter into the most profound nothingness.

I had an internal strife, which continually racked me – two powers which appeared equally strong seemed equally to struggle for the mastery within me. On the one hand, a desire of pleasing Thee, O my God, a fear of offending, and a continual tendency of all my powers to Thee – on the other side, the view of all my inward corruptions, the depravity of my heart, and the continual stirring and rising of self. What torrents of tears, what desolations have these cost me? 'Is it possible,' I cried, 'that I have received so many graces and favours from God only to lose them; – that I have loved Him with so much ardour, but to be eternally deprived of Him; that His benefits have only produced ingratitude; His fidelity been repaid with infidelity; that my heart has been emptied of all creatures, and created objects, and filled with His blessed presence and love, in order now to be wholly void of divine power, and only filled with wanderings and created objects!'

I could now no longer pray as formerly. Heaven seemed shut to me, and I thought justly. I could get no consolation or make any complaint; nor had I any creature on earth to apply to. I found myself banished from all beings without finding a support of refuge in anything. I could no more practise any virtue with facility. 'Alas!' said I, 'is it possible that this heart, formerly all on fire, should now become like ice!' I often thought all creatures combined against me. Laden with a weight of past sins, and a multitude of new ones, I could not think God would ever pardon me, but looked on myself as a victim designed for Hell. I would have been glad to do penances, to make use of prayers, pilgrimages, and vows. But still, whatever I tried for a remedy seemed only to increase the malady. I may say that tears were my drink, and sorrow my food. I felt in myself such a pain as I never could bring any to comprehend, but such as have experienced it. I had within myself an executioner who tortured me without respite. Even when I went to church, I was not easy there. To sermons I could give no attention; they were now of no service or refreshment to me. I scarcely conceived or understood anything in them, or about them.

David Brainerd's Journal

FROM JONATHAN EDWARDS, *LIFE OF BRAINERD*

ی۵In a mournful melancholy state, on July 12, 1739, I was attempting to pray; but found no heart to engage in that or any other duty; my former concern, exercise, and religious affections were now gone. I thought that the Spirit of God had quite left me; but still was not distressed; yet disconsolate, as if there was nothing in heaven or earth could make me happy. Having been thus endeavouring to pray – though, as I thought, very stupid and senseless – for near half an hour; then, as I was walking in a thick grove, unspeakable glory seemed to open to the apprehension of my soul. I do not mean any external brightness, nor any imagination of a body of light, but it was a new inward apprehension or view that I had of God, such as I never had before, nor anything which had the least resemblance to it. I had no particular apprehension of any one person in the Trinity, either the Father, the Son, or the Holy Spirit; but it appeared to be Divine glory.

My soul rejoiced with joy unspeakable, to see such a God, such a glorious Divine Being; and I was inwardly pleased and satisfied that he should be God over all for ever and ever. My soul was so captivated and delighted with the excellency of God that I was even swallowed up in him; at least to that degree that I had no thought about my own salvation, and scarce reflected that there was such a creature as myself. I continued in this state of inward joy, peace, and astonishing, till near dark without any abatement; and then began to think and examine what I had seen; and felt sweetly composed in my mind all the evening following. I felt myself in a new world, and everything about me appeared with a different aspect from what it was wont to do.

FROM DAVID BRAINERD'S *JOURNAL*
August 7, 1745

୶Preached to the Indians from Isaiah 53:3–10. There was a remarkable influence attending the word, and great concern in the assembly. Most were much affected and in great distress for their souls; and some few could neither go nor stand, but lay flat on the ground, as if pierced at heart, crying incessantly for mercy. Several were newly awakened, and it was remarkable, that as fast as they came from remote places round about, the Spirit of God seemed to seize them with concern for their souls.

August 8, 1745

୶In the afternoon I preached to the Indians; their number was about sixty-five people, men, women and children. I spoke from Luke 14:16–23 and was favoured with uncommon freedom in my discourse. There was much visible concern among them while I was speaking, but afterwards when I spoke with them individually, the power of God seemed to descend on the assembly 'like rushing mighty wind', and with an astonishing energy bore down all before it.

I stood amazed at the influence that seized the audience almost universally, and could compare it to nothing more aptly than the irresistible force of a mighty torrent or swelling deluge, that with its insupportable weight and pressure bears down and sweeps before it whatever is in its way. Almost everyone, of all ages, were bowed down with concern together, and hardly anyone was able to withstand the shock of this surprising work. Old men and women who had been drunken wretches for many years, and some little children not more than six or seven years of age, appeared in distress for their souls, as well as middle-aged people.

A leader among the Indians who had been previously most self-righteous told me, 'he had been a Christian more than ten years' but was now brought under a solemn concern for his soul, and wept bitterly. Another man, advanced in years, who had been a murderer, a powwow (conjurer), and a notorious drunkard now cried with many tears for God's mercy.

There was one remarkable instance of awakening this day, that I cannot but take particular notice of here. A young Indian woman, who I believe never knew before she had a soul, nor ever thought of any such thing, hearing that there was something strange among the Indians, came it seems to see what was the matter. On her way to the Indians she called at my lodgings, and when I told her I intended to shortly preach to the Indians she laughed. Nevertheless she joined them. By the time I had finished preaching she was so convinced about her sin and misery, and so distressed about her soul's salvation, that she seemed like one pierced through with a dart, and cried out incessantly.

She could neither go nor stand, nor sit on her seat without being held up. After the service was over she lay flat on the ground praying earnestly, and would take no notice of, nor give any answer to, anyone who spoke to her. I tried to listen to what she said, and perceived that the burden of her prayer was, *Guttummaukalummeh wechaumeh melch Ndah*, that is, 'Have mercy on me, and help me to give you my heart.' She continued to pray like this for hour upon hour. This was indeed a surprising day of God's power and seemed enough to convince an atheist of the truth and importance, and power of God's word.

My baptism in the Holy Spirit

W.R. MOODY, *THE LIFE OF D.L MOODY*

I began to cry as never before, for a greater blessing from God. The hunger increased; I really felt that I did not want to live any longer. [Although he was a Christian, a minister, and saw people being converted, he wanted more people to be converted.] I kept on crying all the time that God would fill me with his Spirit. Well, one day in the city of New York – oh! what a day, I cannot describe it, I seldom refer to it. It is almost too sacred an experience to name. Paul had an experience of which he never spoke for 14 years. I can only say, God revealed himself to me, and I had such an experience of his love that I had to ask him to stay his hand. I went preaching again. The sermons were not different; I did not present any new truths, and yet hundreds were converted. I would not now be placed back where I was before that blessed experience if you should give me all the world – it would be small dust in the balance.

ALLEGORIES AND STORIES

⁓◦⦿◦⁓

St Francis' command

THE LITTLE FLOWERS OF ST FRANCIS OF ASSISI
How St Francis, having allowed an evil thought to arise in his mind
against Brother Bernard, ordered him to place his foot three times
upon his neck and his mouth

⁓St Francis, the devoted servant of the crucified Jesus, through constant weeping and penance, had become nearly blind, so that he could scarcely see. Wishing one day to speak with Brother Bernard on things divine, he left the place where he was and went to join him. Being told, upon arrival, that he was in the forest praying, St Francis proceeded thither, and, calling out, said, 'Come, O Brother Bernard, and speak with this blind man.'

But Brother Bernard did not make answer; for, his soul being rapt in divine contemplation, he did not hear him call; one of the special graces of Brother Bernard being that of holding converse with God Almighty, of which St Francis had often been a witness. The saint, therefore, since he wished specially to speak with him at that hour, called him again a second time and a third. Brother Bernard, not having heard him, neither answered nor went to him; at which St Francis went away somewhat saddened, and wondering in himself how it was that, having called him three times, Brother Bernard had not come to him. With this thought on his mind, when he had proceeded a little way, he bade his companion wait for him, and retiring to a solitary spot, fell on his knees, praying that God would reveal to him why Brother Bernard had not answered his call. As he prayed, a voice came from God, which said, 'O poor little man, why art thou troubled? Is it meet for man to leave God for the creature? When thou didst call Brother Bernard he was with me, and could neither hear thee, nor go to thee; be not then surprised if he answered thee not, for he was rapt out of himself, nor did he hear aught of all thou saidst.'

St Francis, having received this answer from God, went back with great haste to Brother Bernard, to accuse himself humbly of the thought he had allowed to enter his mind against him. Brother Bernard, seeing St Francis coming towards him, went to meet him, and threw himself at his feet. Then St Francis bade him rise, confessing most humbly what his thoughts had been and the answer which God had made him; and with these words he concluded: 'I command thee, by virtue of holy obedience, to do whatsoever I shall order thee.'

Brother Bernard, fearing St Francis would oblige him to inflict upon him some great punishment, as was his custom, would most willingly have avoided obeying him. 'I am ready,' he answered, 'to obey thee, father, if thou also wilt promise me to do whatsoever I shall command thee.'

To this St Francis consented; and Brother Bernard then asked him what he wished him to do. 'I command thee,' said St Francis, 'under holy obedience, in order to punish my presumption and the evil thought of my heart, when I lie down on the ground to place one of thy feet on my neck, and the other on my mouth.

And this shalt thou do thee! Be humbled, thou son of Peter Bernardoni, for thou art but a vile wretch; how camest thou to be so proud, thou miserable servant of sin!'

On hearing this Brother Bernard was much grieved, but out of holy obedience he did what St Francis had ordered him, striving withal to acquit himself thereof as lightly as possible. Then St Francis, having promised obedience to Brother Bernard, asked what he wished him to do, whereto the latter answered: 'I command thee, in virtue of holy obedience, that whenever we are together thou reprove and correct with great severity all my defects.' This order much surprised St Francis, for Brother Bernard was so holy that he held him in great reverence, and did not believe it possible to find in him any fault. From that time, therefore, the saint avoided being much with Brother Bernard, fearing lest, out of holy obedience, he might be obliged to reprove him; and when he was obliged to see or to speak with him, he parted from him as soon as possible. Most edifying it was to hear with what charity, what admiration and humility, St Francis, who was his superior, spoke of Brother Bernard, who was his first son in God – to the praise and glory of Jesus Christ and his poor servant Francis. Amen.

Pilgrim starts his journey

JOHN BUNYAN, *THE PILGRIM'S PROGRESS*
✍As I walked through the wilderness of this world, I lighted on a certain place where was a den, and laid me down in that place to sleep; and as I slept, I dreamed a dream. I dreamed, and behold, I saw a man clothed with rags, standing in a certain place, with his face from his own house, a book in his hand, and a great burden upon his back. (Isaiah 64:6; Luke 14:33; Psalm 38:4). I

looked and saw him open the book, and read therein; and as he read, he wept and trembled; and not being able longer to contain, he brake out with a lamentable cry, saying, 'What shall I do?' (Acts 2:37; 16:30; Habakkuk 1:2, 3.)

In this plight, therefore, he went home, and restrained himself as long as he could, that his wife and children should not perceive his distress; but he could not be silent long, because that his trouble increased. Wherefore at length he brake his mind to his wife and children; and thus he began to talk to them: 'O, my dear wife,' said he, 'and you the children of my bowels, I, your dear friend, am in myself undone by reason of a burden that lieth hard upon me; moreover, I am certainly informed that this our city will be burnt with fire from heaven; in which fearful overthrow, both myself, with thee my wife, and you my sweet babes, shall miserably come to ruin, except (the which yet I see not) some way of escape can be found whereby we may be delivered.' At this his relations were sore amazed; not for that they believed that what he had said to them was true, but because they thought that some frenzy distemper had got into his head; therefore, it drawing towards night, and they hoping that sleep might settle his brains, with all haste they got him to bed. But the night was as troublesome to him as the day; wherefore, instead of sleeping, he spent it in sighs and tears. So when the morning was come, they would know how he did. He told them, 'Worse and worse': he also set to talking to them again; but they began to be hardened. They also thought to drive away his distemper by harsh and surly carriage to him; sometimes they would deride, sometimes they would chide, and sometimes they would quite neglect him. Wherefore he began to retire himself to his chamber to pray for and pity them, and also to condole his own misery; he would also walk solitarily in the fields, sometimes reading, and sometimes praying: and thus for some days he spent his time.

Now I saw, upon a time, when he was walking in the fields, that he was (as he was wont) reading in his book, and greatly distressed in his mind; and as he read, he burst out, as he had done before, crying, 'What shall I do to be saved?' (Acts 16:30, 31.)

I saw also that he looked this way, and that way, as if he would run; yet he stood still because (as I perceived) he could not tell which way to go. I looked then, and saw a man named Evangelist coming to him, and he asked, 'Wherefore dost thou cry?'

He answered, 'Sir, I perceive, by the book in my hand, that I am condemned to die, and after that to come to judgement, (Hebrews 9:27); and I find that I am not willing to do the first, (Job 10: 21, 22), nor able to do the second.' (Ezekiel 22:14).

Then said Evangelist, 'Why not willing to die, since this life is attended with so many evils?' The man answered, 'Because, I fear that this burden that is upon my back will sink me lower than the grave, and I shall fall into Tophet. (Isaiah 30:33). And Sir, if I be not fit to go to prison, I am not fit to go to judgement, and from thence to execution; and the thoughts of these things make me cry.'

Then said Evangelist, 'If this be thy condition, why standesth thou still?' He answered, 'Because I know not whither to go.' Then he gave him a parchment roll, and there was written within, 'Fly from the wrath to come.' (Matthew 3:7).

The man therefore read it, and looking upon Evangelist very carefully, said, 'Whither must I fly?' Then said Evangelist, (pointing with his finger over a very wide field), 'Do you see yonder wicket-gate?' (Matthew 7:13, 14). The man said, 'No.' Then said the other, 'Do you see yonder shining light?' (Psalm 119:105; 2 Peter 1:19). He said, 'I think I do.' Then said Evangelist, 'Keep that light in your eye, and go up directly thereto, so shalt thou see the gate; at which, when thou knockest, it shall be told thee what thou shalt do.' So I saw in my dream that the man began to run.

Now he had not run far from his own door when his wife and children, perceiving it, began to cry after him to return; but the man put his fingers in his ears, and ran on crying, Life! life! eternal life! (Luke 14:26). So he looked not behind him, (Genesis 19:17), but fled towards the middle of the plain.

Christian loses his burden

JOHN BUNYAN, *THE PILGRIM'S PROGRESS*

∾Now I saw in my dream, that the highway up which Christian was to go, was fenced on either side with a wall, and that wall was called Salvation. (Isaiah 26:1). Up this way, therefore, did burdened Christian run, but not without great difficulty, because of the load on his back.

He ran thus till he came at a place somewhat ascending; and upon that place stood a cross, and a little below, in the bottom, a sepulchre. So I saw in my dream, that just as Christian came up with the cross, his burden loosed from off his shoulders, and fell from off his back, and began to tumble, and so continued to do till it came to the mouth of the sepulchre, where it fell in, and I saw it no more.

Then was Christian glad and lightsome, and said with a merry heart, 'He hath given me rest by his sorrow, and life by his death.' Then he stood still a while, to look and wonder; for it was very surprising to him that the sight of the cross should thus ease him of his burden. He looked, therefore, and looked again, even till the springs that were in his head sent the waters down his cheeks. (Zechariah 12:10). Now as he stood looking and weeping, behold, three Shining Ones came to him, and saluted him with, 'Peace be to thee.' So the first said to him, 'Thy sins be forgiven thee,' (Mark 2:5); the second stripped him of his rags, and clothed him with change of raiment, (Zechariah 3:4); the third also set a mark on his forehead, (Ephesians 1:13), and gave him a roll with a seal upon it, which he bid him look on as he ran, and that he should give it in at the celestial gate: so they went their way. Then Christian gave three leaps for joy, and went on singing,

'Thus far did I come laden with my sin,
Nor could aught ease the grief that I was in,
Till I came hither. What a place is this!
Must here be the beginning of my bliss?
Must here the burden fall from off my back?
Must here the strings that bound it to me crack?
Blest cross! blest sepulchre! blest rather be
The Man that there was put to shame for me!'

Doubting Castle and Giant Despair

JOHN BUNYAN, *THE PILGRIM'S PROGRESS*

∪Wherefore at last, lighting under a little shelter, they sat down there till the day brake; but being weary, they fell asleep. Now there was, not far from the place where they lay, a castle, called Doubting Castle, the owner whereof was Giant Despair, and it was in his grounds they now were sleeping: wherefore he, getting up in the morning early, and walking up and down in his fields, caught Christian and Hopeful asleep in his grounds. Then with a grim and surly voice, he bid them awake, and asked them whence they were, and what they did in his grounds. They told him they were pilgrims, and that they had lost their way. Then said the giant, You have this night trespassed on me by trampling in and lying on my grounds, and therefore you must go along with me. So they were forced to go, because he was stronger than they.

They also had but little to say, for they knew themselves in a fault. The giant, therefore, drove them before him, and put them into his castle, into a very dark dungeon, nasty and stinking to the spirits of these two men. Here, then, they lay from Wednesday morning till Saturday night, without one bit of bread, or drop of drink, or light, or any to ask how they did; they were, therefore, here in evil case, and were far from friends and acquaintance. (Psalm 88:18). Now in this place Christian had double sorrow, because it was through his unadvised counsel that they were brought into this distress.

Now Giant Despair had a wife, and her name was Diffidence: so when he was gone to bed he told his wife what he had done, to wit, that he had taken a couple of prisoners, and cast them into his dungeon for trespassing on his grounds. Then he asked her also what he had best do further to them. So she asked him what they were, whence they came, and whither they were bound, and he told her. Then she counselled him, that when he arose in the morning he should beat them without mercy. So when he arose, he getteth him a grievous crab-tree cudgel, and goes down into the dungeon to them, and there first falls to rating of them as if they were dogs, although they gave him never a word of distaste. Then he falls upon them, and beats them fearfully, in such sort that they were not able to help themselves, or to turn them upon the floor. This done, he withdraws and leaves them there to condole their misery, and to mourn under their distress: so all that day they spent the time in nothing but sighs and bitter lamentations. The next night, she, talking with her husband further about them, and understanding that they were yet alive, did advise him to counsel them to make away with themselves. So when morning was come, he goes to them in a surly manner, as before, and perceiving them to be very sore with the stripes that he had given them the day before, he told them, that since they were never like to come out of that place, their only way would be forthwith to make an end of themselves, either with knife, halter, or poison; for why, said he, should you choose to live, seeing it is attended with so much bitterness? But they desired him to let them go. With that he looked ugly upon them, and rushing to them, had doubtless made an end of them himself, but that he fell into one of his fits (for he sometimes in sunshiny weather fell into fits), and lost for a time the use of his hands; wherefore he withdrew, and left them as before to consider what to do. Then did the prisoners consult between themselves whether it was best to take his counsel or no; and thus they began to discourse:

CHR. Brother, said Christian, what shall we do? The life that we now live is miserable. For my part, I know not whether it is best to live thus, or to die out of hand. My soul chooseth strangling rather than life, and the grave is more easy for me than this dungeon. (Job 7:15). Shall we be ruled by the giant?

HOPE. Indeed our present condition is dreadful, and death would be far more welcome to me than thus for ever to abide; but yet, let us consider, the Lord of the country to which we are going hath said, 'Thou shalt do no murder,' no, not to another man's person; much more, then, are we forbidden to take his counsel to kill ourselves. Besides, he that kills another, can but commit murder upon his body; but for one to kill himself, is to kill body and soul at once. And moreover, my brother, thou talkest of ease in the grave; but hast thou forgotten the hell whither for certain the murderers go? for 'no murderer hath eternal life,' etc. And let us consider again, that all the law is not in the hand of Giant Despair: others, so far as I can understand, have been taken by him as well as we, and yet have escaped out of his hands. Who knows but that God, who made the world, may cause that Giant Despair may die; or that, at some time or other, he may forget to lock us in; or that he may, in a short time, have another of his fits before us, and may lose the use of his limbs? And if ever that should come to pass again, for my part, I am resolved to pluck up the heart of a man, and to try my utmost to get from under his hand. I was a fool that I did not try to do it before. But, however, my brother, let us be patient, and endure a while: the time may come that may give us a happy release; but let us not be our own murderers. With these words Hopeful at present did moderate the mind of his brother; so they continued together in the dark that day, in their sad and doleful condition.

Well, towards evening the giant goes down into the dungeon again, to see if his prisoners had taken his counsel. But when he came there he found them alive; and truly, alive was all; for now, what for want of bread and water, and by reason of the wounds they received when he beat them, they could do little but breathe. But I say, he found them alive; at which he fell into a grievous rage, and told them, that seeing they had disobeyed his counsel, it should be worse with them than if they had never been born.

At this they trembled greatly, and I think that Christian fell into a swoon; but coming a little to himself again, they renewed their discourse about the giant's counsel, and whether yet they had best take it or no. Now Christian again seemed for doing it; but Hopeful made his second reply as followeth:

HOPE. My brother, said he, rememberest thou not how valiant thou hast been heretofore? Apollyon could not crush thee, nor could all that thou didst hear, or see, or feel, in the Valley of the Shadow of Death. What hardship, terror, and amazement hast thou already gone through; and art thou now nothing but fears! Thou seest that I am in the dungeon with thee, a far weaker man by nature than thou art. Also this giant hath wounded me as well as thee, and hath also cut off the bread and water from my mouth, and with thee I mourn without the light. But let us exercise a little more patience. Remember how thou playedst the man at Vanity Fair, and wast neither afraid of the chain nor cage, nor yet of bloody death: wherefore let us (at least to avoid the shame that it becomes not a Christian to be found in) bear up with patience as well as we can.

Now night being come again, and the giant and his wife being in bed, she asked him concerning the prisoners, and if they had taken his counsel: to which he replied, They are sturdy rogues; they choose rather to bear all hardships than to make away with themselves. Then said she, Take them into the castle-yard to-morrow, and show them the bones and skulls of those that thou hast already dispatched, and make them believe, ere a week comes to an end, thou wilt tear them in pieces, as thou hast done their fellows before them.

So when the morning was come, the giant goes to them again, and takes them into the castle-yard, and shows them as his wife had bidden him. These, said he, were pilgrims, as you are, once, and they trespassed on my grounds, as you have done; and when I thought fit I tore them in pieces; and so within ten days I will do you: get you down to your den again. And with that he beat them all the way thither. They lay, therefore, all day on Saturday in a lamentable case, as before. Now, when night was come, and when Mrs. Diffidence and her husband the giant was got to bed, they began to renew their discourse of their prisoners; and withal, the old giant wondered that he could neither by his blows nor counsel bring them to an end. And with that his wife replied, I fear, said she, that they live in hopes that some will come to relieve them; or that they have picklocks about them, by the means of which they hope to escape. And sayest thou so, my dear? said the giant; I will therefore search them in the morning.

Well, on Saturday, about midnight they began to pray, and continued in prayer till almost break of day.

Now, a little before it was day, good Christian, as one half amazed, brake out into this passionate speech: What a fool, quoth he, am I, thus to lie in a stinking dungeon, when I may as well walk at liberty! I have a key in my bosom, called Promise, that will, I am persuaded, open any lock in Doubting Castle. Then said Hopeful, That is good news; good brother, pluck it out of thy bosom, and try.

Then Christian pulled it out of his bosom, and began to try at the dungeon-door, whose bolt, as he turned the key, gave back, and the door flew open with ease, and Christian and Hopeful both came out. Then he went to the outward door that leads into the castle-yard, and with his key opened that door also. After he went to the iron gate, for that must be opened too; but that lock went desperately hard, yet the key did open it. They then thrust open the gate to make their escape with speed; but that gate, as it opened, made such a creaking, that it waked Giant Despair, who hastily rising to pursue his prisoners, felt his limbs to fail, for his fits took him again, so that he could by no means go after them. Then they went on, and came to the King's highway, and so were safe, because they were out of his jurisdiction.

POETRY

⚬⚬⚬⚬

The Lord is my shepherd

PSALM 23 NRSV

The Lord is my shepherd, I shall not want.
* He makes me lie down in green pastures;*
he leads me beside still waters;
* he restores my soul.*
He leads me in right paths
* for his name's sake.*

Even though I walk through the darkest valley,
* I fear no evil;*
for you are with me;
* your rod and your staff –*
* they comfort me.*

You prepare a table before me
* in the presence of my enemies;*
you anoint my head with oil;
* my cup overflows.*

Surely goodness and mercy shall follow me
all the days of my life,
and I shall dwell in the house of the Lord
my whole life long.

Bless the Lord, O my soul

PSALM 103:1–5 NRSV
Bless the Lord, O my soul,
and all that is within me,
bless his holy name.
Bless the Lord, O my soul,
and do not forget all his benefits –
who forgives all your iniquity,
who heals all your diseases,
who redeems your life from the Pit,
who crowns you with steadfast love and mercy,
who satisfies you with good as long as you live
so that your youth is renewed like the eagle's.

Most glorious Lord of Life

EDMUND SPENSER
Most glorious Lord of Life! that, on this day
Didst make thy triumph over death and sin;
And, having harrowed hell, didst bring away
Captivity thence captive, us to win:
This joyous day, dear Lord, with joy begin;
And grant that we, for whom thou didst die,
Being with thy dear blood clean washed from sin,

May live for ever in felicity!
And that thy love we weighing worthily,
May likewise love thee for the same again;
And for thy sake, that all like dear didst buy,
With love may one another entertain!
  So let us love, dear Love, like as we ought.
  — Love is the lesson which the Lord us taught.

Hear me, O God!

BEN JONSON, *THE UNDERWOOD*, POEMS OF DEVOTION
Hear me, O God!
  A broken heart
  Is my best part:
Use still thy rod,
  That I may prove
  Therein thy love.

If thou hadst not
  Been stern to me,
  But left me free,
I had forgot
  Myself and thee.

For sin's so sweet,
  As minds ill bent
  Rarely repent,
Until they meet
  Their punishment.

Who more can crave
   Than thou hast done?
   That gav'st a Son,
To free a slave
   First made of nought;
   With all since bought.

Sin, death, and hell
   His glorious name
   Quite overcame,
Yet I rebel,
   And slight the same.

But I'll come in,
   Before my loss
   Me farther toss,
As sure to win
   Under his cross.

Wilt Thou forgive that sin where I begun

JOHN DONNE

Wilt Thou forgive that sin where I begun,
   Which is my sin, though it were done before?
Wilt Thou forgive that sin through which I run,
   And do run still, though still I do deplore?
     When Thou hast done, Thou hast not done,
      For I have more.

Wilt Thou forgive that sin which I have won
   Others to sin? and made my sin their door?
Wilt Thou forgive that sin which I did shun

A year or two, but wallowed in, a score?
When Thou hast done, Thou hast not done,
For I have more.

I have a sin of fear, that when I have spun
My last thread, I shall perish on the shore;
Swear by Thyself, that at my death Thy Son
Shall shine as He shines now and heretofore;
And, having done that, Thou hast done,
I fear no more.

Good Friday 1613. Riding Westward

JOHN DONNE

Let man's Soul be a Sphere, and then, in this,
The intelligence that moves, devotion is;
And as the other Spheres, by being grown
Subject to foreign motions, lose their own,
And being by others hurried every day,
Scarce in a year their natural form obey:
Pleasure of business, so, our Souls admit
For their first mover, and are whirled by it.
Hence is't, that I am carried towards the West
This day, when my Soul's form bends towards the East.
There I should see a Sun, by rising set,
And by that setting endless day beget;
But that Christ on this Cross, did rise and fall,
Sin had eternally benighted all.
Yet dare I almost be glad, I do not see
That spectacle of too much weight for me.
Who sees God's face, that is self life, must die;

What a death were it then to see God die?
It made his own Lieutenant Nature shrink,
It made his footstool crack, and the Sun wink.
Could I behold those hands which span the Poles,
And tune all spheres at once, pierc'd with those holes?
Could I behold that endless height which is
Zenith to us, and our Antipodes,
Humbled below us? or that blood which is
The seat of all our Souls, if not of his,
Made dirt of dust, or that flesh which was worn
By God, for his apparel, ragg'd, and torn?
If on these things I durst not look, durst I
Upon his miserable mother cast mine eye,
Who was God's partner here, and furnish'd thus
Half of that Sacrifice, which ransom'd us?
Though these things, as I ride, be from mine eye,
They are present yet unto my memory,
For that looks towards them; and thou look'st towards me,
O Saviour, as Thou hang'st upon the tree;
I turn my back to Thee, but to receive
Corrections, till Thy mercies bid Thee leave.
O think me worth Thine anger, punish me,
Burn off my rusts, and my deformity,
Restore Thine Image, so much, by Thy grace,
That Thou may'st know me, and I'll turn my face.

Sonnet X

JOHN DONNE
Death be not proud, though some have callèd thee
Mighty and dreadful, for thou art not so;

For those whom thou thinkst thou dost overthrow
Die not, poor death, nor yet canst thou kill me;
From rest and sleep, which but thy pictures be,
Much pleasure, then from thee, much more must flow,
And soonest our best men with thee do go,
Rest of their bones, and soul's delivery.
Thou art slave to fate, chance, kings, and desperate men,
And dost with poison, war, and sickness dwell;
And poppy or charms can make us sleep as well
And better than thy stroke; why swellst thou then?
One short sleep past, we wake eternally,
And death shall be no more: death thou shalt die.

The God of love my shepherd is

GEORGE HERBERT, *THE TEMPLE*

The God of love my shepherd is,
  And he that doth me feed:
While he is mine, and I am His,
  What can I want or need?

He leads me to the tender grass,
  Where I both feed and rest;
Then to the streams that gently pass:
  In both I have the best.

Or if I stray, he doth convert,
  And bring my mind in frame:
And all this not for my desert,
  But for his holy name.

Yea, in death's shady, black abode
  Well may I walk, not fear:
For thou art with me, and thy rod
  To guide, thy staff to bear.

Nay, thou dost make me sit and dine,
  Even in my enemies' sight;
My head with oil, my cup with wine
  Runs over day and night.

Surely thy sweet and wondrous love
  Shall measure all my days;
And as it never shall remove,
  So neither shall my praise.

Love

GEORGE HERBERT

Love bade me welcome: yet my soul drew back,
  Guilty of dust and sin.
But quick-ey'd Love, observing me grow slack
  From my first entrance in,
Drew nearer to me, sweetly questioning,
  If I lack'd any thing.

'A guest', I answer'd, ' worthy to be here.'
  Love said, 'You shall be he.'
'I the unkind, ungrateful? Ah my dear,
  I cannot look on thee.'
Love took my hand, and smiling did reply,
  'Who made the eyes but I?'

'Truth Lord, but I have marr'd them: let my shame
  Go where it doth deserve.'
'And know you not', says Love, 'who bore the blame?'
  'My dear, then I will serve.'
'You must sit down,' says Love, 'and taste my meat.'
  So I did sit and eat.

Let all the world in every corner sing

GEORGE HERBERT

Let all the world in every corner sing,
'My God and King!'
The heavens are not too high,
His praise may thither fly:
The earth is not too low,
His praises there may grow,
The church with psalms must shout,
No door can keep them out:
But, above all, the heart
Must bear the longest part.
Let all the world in every corner sing,
'My God and King!'

My words and thoughts do both express
this notion

GEORGE HERBERT, *THE TEMPLE*, COLOSSIANS 3:3
My words and thoughts do both express this notion,
That Life hath with the sun a double motion.
The first Is straight, and our diurnal friend;

The other Hid, and doth obliquely bend.
One life is wrapt In flesh, and tends to earth:
The other winds towards Him, whose happy birth
Taught me to live here so That still one eye
Should aim and shoot at that which Is on high;
Quitting with daily labour all My pleasure,
To gain at harvest an eternal Treasure.

Easter Wings

GEORGE HERBERT, *THE TEMPLE*

Lord, who createdst man in wealth and store,
Though foolishly he lost the same,
Decaying more and more,
Till he became
Most poor:
With thee
Oh let me rise
As larks, harmoniously,
And sing this day thy victories:
Then shall the fall farther the flight in me.
My tender age in sorrow did begin:
And still with sickness and shame
Thou did'st so punish sin,
That I became
Most thin.
With thee
Let me combine,
And feel this day the victory,
For, if I imp my wing on thine,
Affliction shall advance the flight in me.

Heaven

GEORGE HERBERT, *THE TEMPLE*

O Who will show me those delights on high?
                    ECHO   *I.*
Thou Echo, thou art mortal, all men know.
                    ECHO   *No.*
Wert thou not born among the trees and leaves?
                    ECHO   *Leaves.*
And are there any leaves, that still abide?
                    ECHO   *Bide.*
What leaves are they? Impart the matter wholly.
                    ECHO   *Holy.*
And holy leaves the Echo then of bliss?
                    ECHO   *Yes.*
Then tell me, what is that supreme delight?
                    ECHO   *Light.*
Light to the mind: what shall the will enjoy?
                    ECHO   *Joy.*
But are there cares and business with the pleasure?
                    ECHO   *Leisure.*
Light, joy, and leisure; but shall they persever?
                    ECHO   *Ever.*

Rex Tragicus

ROBERT HERRICK, *REX TRAGICUS*, OR *CHRIST GOING TO HIS CROSS*

[The poet, as he watches the scene in his imagination, addresses Christ.]

Put off thy robe of purple, then go on
To the sad place of execution:
Thine hour is come; and the tormentor stands
Ready, to pierce thy tender feet, and hands.
Long before this, the base, the dull, the rude,
Th'inconstant and unpurged multitude
Yawn for thy coming; some ere this time cry,
How he defers, how loath he is to die!
Amongst this scum, the soldier with his spear,
And that sour fellow, with his vinegar,
His sponge, and stick, do ask why thou dost stay?
So do the scurf and bran too: Go thy way,
Thy way, thou guiltless Man, and satisfy
By thine approach, each their beholding eye.
Not as a thief, shalt thou ascend the mount,
But like a person of some high account:
The cross shall be thy stage; and thou shalt there
The spacious field have for thy theatre.
Thou art that Roscius, and that marked-out man,
That must this day act the tragedian,
To wonder and affrightment: Thou art He,
Whom all the flux of nations comes to see;
Not those poor thieves that act their parts with Thee:
Those act without regard, when once a King,
And God, as thou art, comes to suffering.
No, no, this scene from thee takes life and sense,
And soul and spirit, plot and excellence.
Then begin, great King! ascend thy throne,
And thence proceed to act thy passion
To such a height, to such a period raised,
As hell, and earth, and heaven may stand amazed.
God, and good angels guide thee; and so bless

Thee in thy several parts of bitterness;
That those, who see thee nailed unto the tree,
May (though they scorn Thee) praise and pity Thee.
And we (Thy lovers) while we see Thee keep
The laws of action, will both sigh and weep;
And bring our spices, and embalm Thee dead;
That done, we'll see Thee sweetly buried.

On his blindness

JOHN MILTON

When I consider how my light is spent
  Ere half my days, in this dark world and wide,
  And that one talent which is death to hide
  Lodged with me useless, though my soul more bent
To serve therewith my Maker, and present
  My true account, lest he returning chide:
  'Doth God exact day-labour, light denied?'
  I fondly ask. But patience, to prevent
That murmur, soon replies: 'God doth not need
  Either man's work or his own gifts, who best
  Bear his mild yoke, they serve him best, his State
Is Kingly. Thousands at his bidding speed
  And post o'er land and ocean without rest;
  They also serve, who only stand and wait.'

He that is down needs fear no fall

JOHN BUNYAN, *THE PILGRIM'S PROGRESS*
He that is down needs fear no fall
He that is low, no pride:
He that is humble ever shall
Have God to be his guide.

I am content with what I have,
Little be it or much:
And, Lord, contentment still I crave,
Because thou savest such.

I was a stricken deer

WILLIAM COWPER, *THE TASK*
[In his mental illness, William Cowper finds he is not alone.]

I was a stricken deer, that left the herd
Long since; with many an arrow deep infixt
My panting side was charg'd, when I withdrew
To seek a tranquil death in distant shades.
There was I found by One who had Himself
Been hurt by th'archers. In His side He bore,
And in His hands and feet, the cruel scars.
With gentle force soliciting the darts,
He drew them forth, and heal'd, and bade me live.
Since then, with few associates, in remote
And silent woods, I wander, far from those
My former partners of the peopled scene;
With few associates, and not wishing more.

My Baptismal Birthday

SAMUEL TAYLOR COLERIDGE

[Coleridge wrote that this poem was 'composed on a sick-bed, under severe bodily suffering, on my spiritual birthday, 28 October'.]

God's child in Christ adopted, – Christ my all, –
What that earth boasts were not lost cheaply, rather
Than forfeit that blest name, by which I call
The Holy One, the Almighty God, my Father? –
Father! in Christ we live, and Christ in Thee –
Eternal Thou, and everlasting we.
The heir of heaven, henceforth I fear not death:
In Christ I live! in Christ I draw the breath
Of the true life! – Let then earth, sea, and sky
Make war against me! On my heart I show
Their mighty master's seal. In vain they try
To end my life, that can but end its woe. –
Is that a death-bed where a Christian lies? –
Yes! but not his – 'tis Death itself there dies.

Pied Beauty

GERARD MANLEY HOPKINS

Glory be to God for dappled things –
  For skies of couple-colour as a brinded cow;
    For rose-moles all in stipple upon trout that swim;
Fresh-firecoal chestnut-falls; finches' wings;
  Landscape plotted and pieced – fold, fallow and plough;
    And áll trádes, their gear and tackle and trim.

All things counter, original, spare, strange;
  Whatever is fickle, freckled (who knows how?)
      With swift, slow; sweet, sour; adazzle, dim;
He fathers-forth whose beauty is past change:
      Praise him.

Easter Monday

CHRISTINA ROSSETTI

Out in the rain a world is growing green,
  On half the trees quick buds are seen
      Where glued-up buds have been.
Out in the rain God's Acre stretches green,
  Its harvest quick tho' still unseen:
      For there the Life hath been.

If Christ hath died His brethren well may die,
  Sing in the gate of death, lay by
      This life without a sigh:
For Christ hath died and good it is to die;
  To sleep when so He lays us by,
      Then wake without a sigh.

Yea, Christ hath died, yea, Christ is risen again:
  Wherefore both life and death grow plain
      To us who wax and wane;
For Christ Who rose shall die no more again:
  Amen: till He makes all things plain
      Let us wax on and wane.

HYMNS

~∞~

Come, Holy Ghost, our souls inspire

ATTRIB JOHN COSIN

Come, Holy Ghost, our souls inspire,
And lighten with celestial fire:
Thou the anointing Spirit art,
Who dost thy sevenfold gifts impart.

Thy blessèd unction from above,
Is comfort, life, and fire of love:
Enable with perpetual light
The dulness of our blinded sight.

Anoint and cheer our soilèd face
With the abundance of thy grace.
Keep far our foes, give peace at home –
Where thou art guide no ill can come.

Teach us to know the Father, Son,
And thee, of both, to be but One;

That, through the ages all along,
This may be our endless song:

Praise to thy eternal merit,
Father, Son, and Holy Spirit.

Litany to the Holy Spirit

ROBERT HERRICK, *LITANY TO THE HOLY SPIRIT*
In the hour of my distress,
When temptations me oppress,
And when I my sins confess,
  Sweet Spirit, comfort me!

When I lie within my bed,
Sick in heart and sick in head,
And with doubts discomforted,
  Sweet Spirit, comfort me!

When the house doth sigh and weep,
And the world is drowned in sleep,
Yet mine eyes the watch do keep,
  Sweet Spirit, comfort me!

When the artless Doctor sees
No one hope but of his fees,
And his skill runs on the lees,
  Sweet Spirit, comfort me!

When the Tempter me pursu'th
With the sins of all my youth,

And half damns me with untruth,
  Sweet Spirit, comfort me!

When the passing bell doth toll,
And the furies in a shoal
Come to fright a parting soul,
  Sweet Spirit, comfort me!

When the tapers now burn blue,
And the comforters are few,
And that number more than true,
  Sweet Spirit, comfort me!

When, God knows, I'm tossed about,
Either with despair, or doubt;
Yet before the glass be out,
  Sweet Spirit, comfort me!

When the judgement is revealed,
And that opened which was sealed,
When to thee I have appealed,
  Sweet Spirit, comfort me!

A Morning Hymn

THOMAS KEN

Awake, my soul, and with the sun
Thy daily stage of duty run;
Shake off dull sloth, and early rise
To pay thy morning sacrifice.

Redeem thy mis-spent time that's past;
Live this day as if 'twere thy last;
T'improve thy talent take due care:
'Gainst the great day thyself prepare.

Let all thy converse be sincere,
Thy conscience as the noonday clear;
Think how all-seeing God thy ways
And all thy secret thoughts surveys.

Influenced by the light divine
Let thy own light in good works shine:
Reflect all heaven's propitious ways,
In ardent love and cheerful praise.

Wake, and lift up thyself, my heart,
And with the angels bear thy part,
Who all night long unwearied sing
Glory to the eternal king.

I wake, I wake, ye heavenly choir;
May your devotion me inspire,
That I like you my age may spend,
Like you may on my God attend.

May I like you in God delight,
Have all day long my God in sight,
Perform like you my Maker's will;
Oh may I never more do ill!

Had I your wings, to heaven I'd fly;
But God shall that defect supply,

And my soul, winged with warm desire,
Shall all day long to heaven aspire.

Glory to Thee who safe has kept,
And hath refreshed me whilst I slept.
Grant, Lord, when I from death shall wake,
I may of endless light partake.

I would not wake, nor rise again,
Even heaven itself I would disdain,
Wert not Thou there to be enjoyed,
And I in hymns to be employed.

Heaven is, dear Lord, where'er Thou art:
Oh never, then, from me depart;
For to my soul 'tis hell to be
But for one moment without Thee.

Lord, I my vows to Thee renew;
Disperse my sins as morning dew;
Guard my first springs of thought and will,
And with Thyself my spirit fill.

Direct, control, suggest, this day,
All I design, or do, or say,
That all my powers, with all their might,
In Thy sole glory may unite.

When I survey the wondrous Cross

ISAAC WATTS

When I survey the wondrous Cross,
  On which the Prince of glory died,
My richest gain I count but loss,
  And pour contempt on all my pride.

Forbid it, Lord, that I should boast
  Save in the death of Christ my God;
All the vain things that charm me most,
  I sacrifice them to his blood.

See from his head, his hands, his feet,
  Sorrow and love flow mingled down;
Did e'er such love and sorrow meet,
  Or thorns compose so rich a crown?

His dying crimson like a robe,
  Spreads o'er his body on the Tree;
Then am I dead to all the globe,
  And all the globe is dead to me.

Were the whole realm of nature mine,
  That were a present far too small;
Love so amazing, so divine,
  Demands my soul, my life, my all.

O happy day, that fixed my choice

ATTRIB PHILIP DODDRIDGE

O happy day, that fixed my choice
On Thee, my Saviour and my God!
Well may this glowing heart rejoice,
And tell its raptures all abroad.

Refrain
O happy day! O happy day! when Jesus washed my sins away!
He taught me how to watch and pray, and live rejoicing every
  day
O happy day! O happy day! when Jesus washed my sins away.

O happy bond, that seals my vows
To Him Who merits all my love!
Let cheerful anthems fill His house,
While to that sacred shrine I move.
Refrain

It's done: the great transaction's done!
I am the Lord's and He is mine;
He drew me and I followed on;
Charmed to confess the voice divine.
Refrain

Now rest, my long divided heart,
Fixed on this blissful centre, rest.
Here have I found a nobler part;
Here heavenly pleasures fill my breast.
Refrain

High heaven, that heard the solemn vow,
That vow renewed shall daily hear,
Till in life's latest hour I bow
And bless in death a bond so dear.
Refrain

Jesu, lover of my soul

CHARLES WESLEY

Jesu, lover of my soul,
  let me to Thy bosom fly,
While the nearer waters roll,
  while the tempest still is high.
Hide me, O my Saviour, hide,
  till the storm of life is past;
Safe into the haven guide,
  O receive my soul at last.

Other refuge have I none,
  hangs my helpless soul on Thee;
Leave, ah! leave me not alone,
  still support and comfort me.
All my trust on Thee is stayed,
  all my help from Thee I bring;
Cover my defenceless head
  with the shadow of Thy wing.

Wilt Thou not regard my call?
  Wilt Thou not accept my prayer?
Lo! I sink, I faint, I fall —
  Lo! on Thee I cast my care;

Reach me out Thy gracious hand!
  While I of Thy strength receive,
Hoping against hope I stand,
  dying, and behold, I live.

Thou, O Christ, art all I want,
  more than all in Thee I find;
Raise the fallen, cheer the faint,
  heal the sick, and lead the blind.
Just and holy is Thy Name,
  I am all unrighteousness;
False and full of sin I am;
  Thou art full of truth and grace.

Plenteous grace with Thee is found,
  grace to cover all my sin;
Let the healing streams abound;
  make and keep me pure within.
Thou of life the fountain art,
  freely let me take of Thee;
Spring Thou up within my heart;
  rise to all eternity.

O for a closer walk with God

WILLIAM COWPER

O for a closer walk with God,
  A calm and heavenly frame;
A light to shine upon the road
  That leads me to the Lamb!

Return, O holy Dove, return,
  Sweet messenger of rest;
I hate the sins that made thee mourn,
  And drove thee from my breast.

The dearest idol I have known,
  Whate'er that idol be,
Help me to tear it from thy throne,
  And worship only thee.

So shall my walk be close with God,
  Calm and serene my frame;
So purer light shall mark the road
  That leads me to the Lamb.

Amazing grace!

JOHN NEWTON

Amazing grace! how sweet the sound
That saved a wretch like me;
I once was lost, but now am found;
Was blind, but now I see.

'Twas grace that taught my heart to fear,
And grace my fear relieved;
How precious did that grace appear,
The hour I first believed!

Through many dangers, toils and snares
I have already come:

'Tis grace that brought me safe thus far,
And grace will lead me home.

The Lord has promised good to me,
His word my hope secures;
He will my shield and portion be
As long as life endures.

Yes, when his heart and flesh shall fail,
And mortal life shall cease,
I shall profess within the veil
A life of joy and peace.

When we've been there a thousand years,
Bright shining as the sun,
We've no less days to sing God's praise
Than when we first begun.

Abide with me

HENRY FRANCIS LYTE

Abide with me; fast falls the eventide;
The darkness deepens; Lord, with me abide:
When other helpers fail, and comforts flee,
Help of the helpless, O abide with me.

Swift to its close ebbs out life's little day;
Earth's joys grow dim, its glories pass away;
Change and decay in all around I see;
O thou who changest not, abide with me.

I need thy presence every passing hour;
What but thy grace can foil the tempter's power?
Who like thyself my guide and stay can be?
Through cloud and sunshine, O abide with me.

I fear no foe with thee at hand to bless;
Ills have no weight, and tears no bitterness.
Where is death's sting? where, grave, thy victory?
I triumph still, if thou abide with me.

Hold thou thy cross before my closing eyes;
Shine through the gloom, and point me to the skies:
Heaven's morning breaks, and earth's vain shadows flee;
In life, in death, O Lord, abide with me!

New every morning

JOHN KEBLE

New every morning is the love
Our wakening and uprising prove;
Through sleep and darkness safely brought,
Restored to life, and power, and thought.

New mercies, each returning day,
Hover around us while we pray;
New perils past, new sins forgiven,
New thoughts of God, new hopes of heaven.

If on our daily course our mind
Be set to hallow all we find,
New treasures still, of countless price,
God will provide for sacrifice.

The trivial round, the common task,
Would furnish all we ought to ask,
Room to deny ourselves, a road
To bring us daily nearer to God.

Only, O Lord, in thy dear love
Fit us for perfect rest above;
And help us this and every day
To live more nearly as we pray.

Praise to the Holiest in the height

JOHN HENRY NEWMAN

Praise to the holiest in the height,
And in the depth be praise;
In all his words most wonderful,
Most sure in all his ways.

O loving wisdom of our God!
When all was sin and shame,
A second Adam to the fight
And to the rescue came.

O wisest love! that flesh and blood,
Which did in Adam fail,
Should strive afresh against the foe,
Should strive and should prevail.

And that a higher gift than grace
Should flesh and blood refine,
God's presence and his very self,
And essence all-divine.

O generous love! that he who smote
In Man, for man, the foe,
The double agony in Man,
For man, should undergo;

And in the garden secretly,
And on the cross on high,
Should teach his brethren, and inspire
To suffer and to die.

Praise to the holiest in the height,
And in the depth be praise;
In all his words most wonderful,
Most sure in all his ways.

Lead, Kindly Light

JOHN HENRY NEWMAN

Lead, kindly light, amid the encircling gloom,
  Lead Thou me on!
The night is dark, and I am far from home –
  Lead Thou me on!
Keep Thou my feet; I do not ask to see
The distant scene – one step enough for me.

I was not ever thus, nor pray'd that Thou
  Shouldst lead me on.
I loved to choose and see my path, but now
  Lead Thou me on!
I loved the garish day, and, spite of fears,
Pride ruled my will: remember not past years.

So long Thy power hath blest me, sure it still
  Will lead me on,
O'er moor and fen, o'er crag and torrent, till
  The night is gone;
And with the morn those angel faces smile
Which I have loved long since, and lost awhile.

Dear Lord and Father of mankind

JOHN GREENLEAF WHITTIER

Dear Lord and Father of mankind,
  Forgive our foolish ways!
Reclothe us in our rightful mind;
In purer lives your service find,
  In deeper reverence, praise.

In simple trust like theirs who heard
  beside the Syrian sea
The gracious calling of the Lord,
Let us, like them, without a word,
  Rise up and follow thee.

O Sabbath rest by Galilee!
  O calm of hills above,
Where Jesus knelt to share with thee
The silence of eternity
  Interpreted by love!

With that deep hush subduing all
  Our words and works that drown
The tender whisper of thy call,

As noiseless let thy blessing fall
  As fell thy manna down.

Drop thy still dews of quietness,
  Till all our strivings cease;
Take from our souls the strain and stress,
And let our ordered lives confess
  The beauty of thy peace.

Breathe through the heats of our desire
  Thy coolness and thy balm;
Let sense be dumb, let flesh retire;
Speak through the earthquake, wind, and fire,
  O still small voice of calm!

In the bleak mid-winter

CHRISTINA ROSSETTI

In the bleak mid-winter
  Frosty wind made moan,
Earth stood hard as iron,
  Water like a stone;
Snow had fallen, snow on snow,
  Snow on snow,
In the bleak mid-winter
  Long ago.

Our God, Heaven cannot hold Him,
  Nor earth sustain;
Heaven and earth shall flee away
  When He comes to reign:

In the bleak mid-winter
  A stable-place sufficed
The Lord God Almighty
  Jesus Christ.

Enough for Him whom cherubim
  Worship night and day,
A breastful of milk
  And a mangerful of hay;
Enough for Him whom angels
  Fall down before,
The ox and ass and camel
  Which adore.

Angels and archangels
  May have gathered there,
Cherubim and seraphim
  Throng'd the air,
But only His mother
  In her maiden bliss
Worshipped the Beloved
  With a kiss.

What can I give Him,
  Poor as I am?
If I were a shepherd
  I would bring a lamb,
If I were a wise man
  I would do my part,
Yet what I can I give Him –
  Give my heart.

INDEX OF AUTHORS
AND SOURCES

❧❧❧

THE 🙵 TIMES

Famous Passages from the Bible

Compiled by Owen Collins

The Authorized Version of the Bible has been in use since 1611 and contains some of the most poignant and striking passages in the English language. This selection of prose and poetry brings them together in one volume to make these words of particular beauty and power more readily accessible.

From the Creation account in Genesis to Christ's Crucifixion and Resurrection, from the reassurance of Psalm 23 to Jeremiah's prophecies of woe, all the most memorable passages from the Bible are here.